ARIS & PHILLIPS HISPANIC CLASSICS

FEDERICO GARCÍA LORCA

Selected Suites

Translated and Introduced by

Roberta Ann Quance

LIVERPOOL UNIVERSITY PRESS

First published 2018 by
Liverpool University Press
4 Cambridge Street
Liverpool
L69 7ZU

www.liverpooluniversitypress.co.uk

British Library Cataloguing-in-Publication data
A British Library CIP record is available

ISBN 978-1-78694-107-7 cased
ISBN 978-1-78694-108-4 paperback

Typeset by Tara Evans
Printed in Poland by BooksFactory.co.uk

Cover image: *Casa de huerta entre dos árboles*, 1923–1925.
Huerta de San Vicente, Casa-Museo Federico García Lorca
(Courtesy of Fundación Federico García Lorca, Madrid/Granada).

CONTENTS

Acknowledgements   v

Introduction   1

Selected Suites

ACKNOWLEDGEMENTS

This project grew out of my experience teaching some of Lorca's *suites* to a small group of students at Queen's University Belfast. I would like to thank early readers who saw samples and remarked on them with enthusiasm, especially Andrés Soria Olmedo and Carol Wilsey. For his sound advice I am indebted, as always, to Carlos Piera, who shares my admiration for Iberian folksong and *arte menor* (though he theorizes *arte mayor*).

Many thanks, finally, to Jonathan Thacker for making room for this book in the series Hispanic Classics.

Roberta Ann Quance
Madrid

INTRODUCTION

'HEART WITHOUT ECHO': LORCA'S *SUITES*

They will lead us, eyes wide open, to the secret nightworld of dreams; to the universes that pulse ineffably over our heads…

Guillaume Apollinaire, 'Poets and the New Spirit of the Times' (1919)

This anthology is based on a series of poems that Federico García Lorca wrote between late 1920 and 1923 and which were first published posthumously in 1983; comprising over 200 poems, they are, to date, one of the least explored corners of the poet's work and one of the most unexpected. They belong to a moment of transition and experimentation, when, having moved from Granada to Madrid, the young writer was brought face to face with the need to move with the times and to leave behind the *modernismo* of his earlier verse. As a newcomer, Lorca needed to make his way among the sometimes strident young avant-gardists, while hoping to win the approval of older masters. The creation of the *suites* was the way he rose to this challenge. They were poems 'in a new mould, with a new aesthetic' (letter, 10 August 1921, *E* 127).[1] But they were also poems which did not find their moment; they were *postergados* [continually postponed]. If Lorca had published them, they would no doubt have taken their place alongside *Canciones* (1927) and the *Poema del cante jondo* (1931) as works that shared a distinct aesthetic. As it happened, they were dispersed among his uncollected work or only partially known down through the years in isolated or selective publication in literary journals, until contemporary editors began to work on them.

Briefly, a *suite* is a group or sequence of short interrelated poems turning on a single theme. Some are reminiscent of haiku and present a series of variations or different perspectives on a subject – for example, *Night*, *Castle of Fireworks*, *Mirror Suite*, *Summer Hours*, *Water Jets*… Yet generally speaking, despite the brevity of most of the poems, the *suites* themselves are

---

1   All references to Lorca's correspondence refer to his *Epistolario completo*, eds Andrew A. Anderson and Christopher Maurer (Madrid: Cátedra, 1997.) I also refer throughout to *Federico García Lorca. Complete Poems* (*CP*), 1st rev. edn Christopher Maurer (New York: Farrar Straus and Giroux, 2002) and *Federico García Lorca, Obras completas* (*OC*), 3 vols, ed. Miguel García-Posada (Barcelona: Galaxia Gutenberg/Círculo de Lectores, 1995–1996).

more complex than a sequence of haiku would allow for. Their subject matter ranges wide: in them we see the lover of nature – who drafted the *Book of Poems* and *Songs* – but we also see a poet questioning the cosmos, desire, time, and human destiny, as if in a kaleidoscope. The individual poems in a *suite* are themselves often fragments, as the modern spirit prescribed, yet they are grouped in a succession that gathers weight. They reflect a poetic that can sit between the visual and the temporal arts. And so, although they often invoke a pictorial or visual aesthetic, they sometimes seem self-consciously to play with the fact that they unfold in time: they may 'ripen' like fields of wheat (*Four Yellow Ballads*), gather and occasionally impede time's flow (*Pools in the Stream*), or they may superimpose one scene upon another (*Palimpsests*). It falls to the reader to find and develop connections between the individual poems in a *suite* and to decide – if the I comes into play at all – whether the poetic subject enunciating the poem is one or, as is more often the case, whether he is sometimes unable to surmount contradiction. Sometimes the pieces in a *suite* offer an elliptical and fragmented narrative: a mock love story (*White Album*) or a journey of poetic exploration (*Blue River*, *The Forest of Clocks*, *In the Garden of the Lunar Grapefruits*). But what we do not see is a poetic subject who explains or interprets or even necessarily inhabits what has been presented in the poems. (Does one inhabit a vision, even of oneself? That is left to the reader to ponder.)

It would seem that for Lorca s*uite* was a flexible term and that his working conception of what it was evolved over the three years in which the project engaged him. In experimenting with this kind of composition, Lorca, who had trained originally as a pianist, may have borrowed the term from musicians such as Debussy, Falla, Albéniz and other composers who had published *suites*. It had served them as a way to gather interrelated pieces on a single theme such as the *Suite Iberia* (1905–1909) by Albéniz or Granados's *Goyescas* (1911). But at one point, at least, Lorca also evoked the Renaissance traditions known as *diferencias* [variations], music composed for the *vihuela* or keyboards.[2] It has been estimated that the fruit of his labours during the three crucial years of 1920–1923 were the over 200 individual

---

2   Christopher Maurer (*CP* 900) notes that in 1926 Lorca briefly entertained the title of *Suites* [Low Sky] for his work, as if to emphasize a mood. But in 1931 in a note in *Poesía española contemporánea 1915–1931*, ed. Gerardo Diego (Madrid: Signo, 1931) Lorca listed as an 'inédito' [unpublished text] the work in verse, *Libro de las diferencias* (p. 299). The term *diferencia* was one he attached to a version of the *suite Remansos* published in a little magazine in 1927. See *OC* I, 850.

poems he left in manuscript, in various stages of completion, destined for a publication that only materialized many years after his death.

On moving to Madrid in 1919, the young poet was immediately challenged by the discovery of avant-garde poetics and set himself two tasks: to bring out his first book of poetry, even though it was already dated in his eyes (the *Libro de poemas* of 1921), and, as he wrote his family, 'to make myself over, continually make myself over [*renovarme, renovarme constantemente*] (18 November, 1920; *E* 88). In the late autumn of 1920 he reported (*E* 93) suffering 'true lyrical fits' [*verdaderos ataques líricos*]; perhaps he was referring to the throes which eventually led to the creation of his first *suites*. For, as he writes to his family (29 March 1921), he has been trying to create a new kind of poetry:

> The struggle that I have ahead of me is an enormous one, for on the one hand I am faced with the old school and on the other hand I have the new school and then I come along, from the very, very new school, making do the best I can with worn out rhythms and things. (*E* 105)

As for the 'new school' – the *ultraístas* and their rivals the *creacionistas* – the moment was a confusing one. Although *Ultra*, with its marked allegiance to Futurism and Dada, was the visible head of the Spanish literary avant-garde, it did not count great poets among its members.[3] It was a grab-bag of ideologies, advocating a poetics that borrowed from all of the *ismos* on offer, provided they went 'beyond' [*ultra*] the nineteenth century. Based in Seville and Madrid, the little magazine *Ultra* disputed theoretical leadership with the small movement of three (approximately) mustered in Spain after the war by the Chilean poet Vicente Huidobro, who as early as 1918 brought French Cubist poetry to the attention of Spaniards. However, Huidobro announced in the first issue of his little magazine *Creación*, which appeared in Madrid in April 1921, that there was no longer any sense in considering rupture the guiding principle of the avant-garde: 'The period of destruction is over; we are now entering the era of creation. [...] This is the cycle of creators and of men who have their hands full of seeds.'[4] This was his way of saying that after Futurism and Dada, the foundations of the old poetry

---

3   But see Juan Manuel Bonet (ed.) for a fair representation, *Las cosas se han roto. Una antología de la poesía ultraísta* (Madrid: Vandalia, 2012).

4   Untitled foreword, *Creación. Revista de arte internacional*, no. 1 (April 1921), 1. The *ultraísta* Guillermo de Torre would date the life span of *ultraísmo* a bit differently, from 1918–1922. See his 'Visita del "Interviewer Ignotus" al autor de *Hélices*', *Revista de Casa América-Galicia* [facsímile edn], 28 (April 1923), pp. 236–38.

were in ruins; on the other hand, something new remained to be made, and the imperative was to create an autonomous object in the poem, one which did not copy reality but aimed to add to it, 'in the way that Nature creates a tree'.[5] The poet could achieve this through the invention of new and startling images that were not chained to mimesis. At this point in history, in poetry as in painting, the artist was enjoined to create a pure art, an art that would be strictly purged of anything excessively 'human' (sentimental, confessional) or led by the 'anecdote' (a storyline).[6] The coming years will see Lorca struggle to keep 'emotion' in his verse without lapsing into the self-exposure he felt could 'kill' his poems, or his poetic voice.[7]

Having established himself as a resident in Madrid and, as we shall see, a participant in its activities, Lorca began to think that he could be part of the renewal that was afoot. As he confides to his family, he has written a 'poematic suite' which he hopes two musician friends (Adolfo Salazar and Robert Gerhard) will set to music, inasmuch as they are 'well initiated into the pure and brand-new schools of art, to which I aspire.' (Maurer notes [*E* 105] that at this time the only poem with 'suite' in the title is *Noche. Suite para piano y voz emocionada* [Night. A Suite for Piano and for a Voice with Feeling].)

A few days later Lorca will send his mother a sample of his experiments as a gift for her saint's day, on 5 April. These poems are, he says, a 'box of poetic chocolates' [*caja de bombones líricos*], consisting of a string of haikus, which he assures his mother are the 'the very last word' [ultísimo grito] in poetry.[8] The previous year the Mexican poet José Juan Tablada had published a fine book of haiku (*Un día*, Caracas, 1919), while Lorca's friend Adolfo Salazar, alert to what had caught on in France, praised a

---

5   See his manifesto, 'Non serviam', reproduced in Gloria Videla, *El ultraísmo. Estudios sobre movimientos poéticos de vanguardia en España*, 2nd ed. (Madrid: Gredos, 1971), 206–208 (p. 207).

6   As early as 1914 José Ortega y Gasset developed his idea of a *poesía 'irrealizada'* [poetry made unreal] in a prologue to the poems of José Moreno Villa, one of the mentors in the Residencia de Estudiantes. See the discussion in Guillermo de Torre, *Literaturas europeas de vanguardia* (1925; Seville: Renacimiento, 2001), 139. In 1925 Ortega would develop the idea of a 'dehumanization' of art in his famous essay of this title, *La deshumanización del arte y otros ensayos* (Madrid: Revista de Occidente, 1998).

7   See a revealing letter to Jorge Guillen (*E* 370) dated 9 September 1926 in which Lorca discusses his poetics with a fellow poet who is a disciple of Paul Valery and 'pure poetry': 'El surtidor no' [Turning on the tap of emotion, no.] See the notes to 'Water Jets' (*Surtidores*) in this volume.

8   See Lorca's cover note to his mother published alongside the poems in the *OC* I, 755–757.

'stellar vibration' in the form. Noting that the poems appeared in a series, he claims that interest in the form did not imply copying its metre but, rather, taking inspiration in its brevity, its power of suggestion.[9] It is worth pointing out that a modernizing poet such as Juan Ramón Jiménez, who published Lorca's first *suites* in his little magazine *Indice* [1921–1922) and whom Lorca regarded as a mentor, had also turned to brief, aphoristic verse.[10]

In the background of Lorca's letters home is a literary ferment born of the conviction among leading writers that the *fin-de-siècle* movement of *modernismo* had been played out and that poetry must renew itself. The literary review *Grecia*, to which Lorca had contributed a sample of his early prose work, *Impresiones y paisajes* [Impressions and Landscapes] (1918), offered an allegory as it moved from the depiction of a classical urn on its cover to an image of a gasoline can beside it, in a paean to the age of speed and the automobile.

The young Lorca quickly found two centres of cultural activity in Madrid: the Ateneo Científico, Literario and Artístico and the Residencia de Estudiantes. Much more has been made of the 'Resi', where Lorca lived from 1919–1928, than the Ateneo.[11] But in his early letters home Lorca reported that he had become a member of the latter and that he was enthusiastic about its library (*E* 59, 64). What's more, Lorca may have found some stimulation in its programme of activities. Founded in 1835, the Ateneo was a haven of liberal opinion and sponsored lectures and events involving people whose work would leave a profound mark on the poet. The leading literary historian Ramón Menéndez Pidal gave the Ateneo's inaugural lecture of 1919–1920 on Spain's early oral lyric, a tradition that would fire the poet's imagination

---

9   In his 'Proposiciones sobre el Hai-kai', *La Pluma* 6 (November 1920), 269–71. Cited in Mario Hernández, 'Introducción', *Primeras canciones. Seis poemas galegos. Poemas sueltos. Colección de canciones populares antiguos* (Madrid: Alianza, 1981), 11–47 (p. 28), who notes that haiku had taken off in France with Paul-Louis Couchoud's *Sages et poètes d'Asie* (1906; 1920). For more on Lorca, see Yong-Tae Min, 'Lorca, poeta oriental', *Cuadernos Hispanoamericanos*, 358 (April 1980), 129–44. On the poetics, see Carlos García Prada, 'La poesía imaginista y el hai-kai japonés', *Revista Iberoamericana* 21, 41 (1956), 373–91 and Pedro Aullón de Haro, *El jaiku en España* (Madrid: Hiperión, 2002).

10   Lorca was involved in unsuccessful plans to host a reception at the Residencia de Estudiantes for the Indian poet Rabindranath Tagore, whom Jiménez's wife Zenobia Camprubí had translated. Tagore cultivated haiku and aphoristic verse. The party had been planned for 28 April 1921. See *E* 110.

11   See, for example, Ian Gibson, *Federico García Lorca* (Barcelona: Grijalbo, 1985), 248, who describes the Residencia as the 'axis' of the poet's life in Madrid between 1919 and 1928.

for years to come.[12] In the library he might have found what would prove to be one of the most important songbooks for Lorca's generation: Francisco Asenjo Barbieri's *Cancionero musical de los siglos XV y XVI* (Madrid: Real Academia de Bellas Artes de San Fernando, 1890), or Pedro Henríquez Ureña's *La versificación irregular en la poesía castellana*, with a prologue by Menéndez Pidal. (Consider that the irregular verse form prevailing in the *suites* is a major difference from the poetic of his first book of poems.)

The Ateneo may, perhaps, even have given him his first taste of vanguardism in action. On the 30 April 1921, it hosted the city's second *ultraísta velada* ('evening festivity'); posters by the Polish *ultraísta* painter Wladislaw Jahl went up like a shout all along the streets of the centre of Madrid.[13]

Conceived as both celebration and provocation, the *ultraísta* event included poetry readings by people Lorca knew as well as a talk by his friend, the Uruguayan artist Rafael Barradas, who had done the costumes and stage settings for his first play, *El maleficio de la mariposa* [The Butterfly's Evil Spell] in March 1920 and also exhibited a portrait of Lorca for an Ateneo show a little later in the month.[14]

Barradas's talk was titled '"El anti-yo": estudio teórico sobre el clownismo, y dibujos en la pizarra' [The anti-self: a theoretical study of clownism, and drawings on the chalkboard]. It is hard to imagine that Lorca would not have been on hand to support his friend against the hostility he was sure to face from the Ateneo's staid audience. Although we do not have the text of Barradas's lecture (there may never have been one), it probably touched on topics that would have struck a chord with the poet – whether he spoke of the clown's masking of emotion or, more philosophically, the role of psychology – if any – in the representation of the self.[15] One critic wrote

12   As noted by Christopher Maurer, *Federico García Lorca y su 'Arquitectura del cante jondo'* (Granada: Comares, 2000), 13. The lecture was held on 29 November 1919.

13   Manuel de la Peña recalls that the event was 'proclaimed to the four corners of the earth by the posters designed by [Wladislaw] Jahl, member of a small Polish avant-garde contingent in Madrid'. See his essay *El ultraísmo en España* (Madrid: Librería Concesionaria Fernando Fe, 1925), no pagination. The first *ultraísta* event had been held on 28 January 1921 at the Parisiana, a well-known night club near the Moncloa, with many 'chicas alegres' [lit. lighthearted girls] devoted to a new night entertainment called the 'soupertango' (suppertango). See a newspaper report quoted in José María Barrera López, *El ultraísmo en Sevilla* (Seville: Alfar, 1987), v.1, 50.

14   Pilar García-Sedas, *Joaquim Torres-García i Rafael Barradas. Un diàleg escrit: 1918– 1928* (Barcelona: Publicacions de l'Abadia de Montserrat, 1994). The author notes (p. 151, n. 4) that among the 29 works shown in the Ateneo in 1920 there was a portrait of Lorca.

15   No text of the talk has been found. See Rafael Santos Torroella, 'Barradas y el *clownismo*',

perceptively that Barradas, a 'cubista a ratos' [an off and on again cubist] sought to capture 'fleeting' impressions, the 'first fruits of perception' in his drawings.[16] Moreover, with his undisguised enthusiasm for a child's point of view, Barradas, like Lorca, looked to child art or children's verse for inspiration.[17] We have only a glimpse of Lorca's curiosity about the early avant-garde, but he is certain to have heard about many more things than he would have let on in his letters home. Madrid's young agitators had taken up residence in the city's cafés and *tertulias*.[18] In the Ateneo, with critic Manuel Abril heading the Art Section, he would have seen or heard about emerging art. There, for example, Rafael Alberti exhibited his early painting – of 'tendencias más avanzadas' – in March 1923.[19] In a letter home from mid-April 1921 Lorca reports that he had entertained two or three *ultraístas* and other friends, including Barradas, the artist and printer Gabriel García Maroto, and the young music critic Adolfo Salazar, in his room at the Residencia (*E* 109) (perhaps Guillermo de Torre was among them). A photograph from the time shows that Lorca was a patron of the Café del Prado, across the street from the Ateneo, where Barradas and others had a *tertulia*.[20] However, café culture was not the kind of activity

in *Rafael Barradas*, exhibition catalogue (Madrid: Galería Jorge Mara, 1992), 25–33, Santos believes it was 'muy posible' (p. 26) that Lorca was there. Existing newspaper reports do not list Lorca among those in attendance, but the coverage is very limited in Madrid.

16   See Francisco Alcántara, 'La vida artística', *El Sol*, 15 de febrero de 1921, p. 3 for a brief review of a later Ateneo show where Barradas exhibited portraits of the actress Catalina Bárcena.

17   See *E* 125. In the middle of his *suites* project the poet laments his 'withered childhood' (*mi niñez seca*) as a wellspring of creativity he thinks is threatened. On Barradas's devotions see Emmanuel Guigon, *La infancia del arte. Arte de los niños y arte moderno en España*. Exhibition catalogue, Museo de Teruel, 5 de noviembre–8 de diciembre; Logroño, Sala Amós Salvador, 13 de diciembre 1996–12 de enero 1997 (Teruel: Museo de Teruel; Logroño: Cultural Rioja. 1996). Barradas illustrated children's books to support his art.

18   Settled into the Residencia on a hill (the *Colina de los Chopos*) in what were then the outskirts of the city, Lorca gave his family to understand that 'Madrid' (the center) was not nearby. In any event the Residencia would probably have seemed more respectable to his family in that it was set apart and the director Jiménez Fraud saw to it that the residents enjoyed the influence of distinguished mentors such as José Moreno Villa, Juan Ramón Jiménez and José Ortega y Gasset.

19   Alberti's first show was announced briefly in *El Sol*, 20 de marzo de 1923, p. 4.

20   The *tertulia* is recalled in Juvenal Ortiz Saralegui, 'Federico García Lorca y Rafael Barradas', *Romance* [México], 19, 18 December 1940, p. 9. A photograph shows Lorca in front of the Café del Prado in the company of Benjamín Jarnés, Humberto Pérez de la Ossa, Rafael Barradas and Luis Buñuel. It is available at http://cvc.cervantes.es/actcult/

Lorca's parents wanted to hear about in their son's letters. They wanted to learn that he was charting his own course (and spending his time wisely).

If we posit an initial moment of curiosity about *ultraísta* activity, through friendship with some of its actors, before he grew disillusioned with its decay, we will imagine Lorca taking in the conversation and the rich oral life that visitors such as Jorge Luis Borges and John Dos Passos had found in Spain.[21] He might also have read the literary journals that were making the transition from modernism to the new art, some of which were sold in the kiosks and others of which were passed from hand to hand. Biographer Ian Gibson suggests for example, that Lorca might have seen an anthology of *ultraísta* poetry in *Cervantes*.[22] Would he not also have read the critical articles and polemics that filled the pages of that journal, or others? On the evidence of the *suites*, Lorca had very little taste for the love of technology and speed which held some *ultraístas* in thrall,[23] nor was he inclined to seek his inspiration in the city, but he did wish to cultivate a new metaphor and a new appreciation for concision. What's more, his own contribution to the newest 'escuela' offered a principle of construction that chimed in a key respect with the avant-garde's aversion to the 'anécdota' [story-line]. In a key article on the latest French verse, Torres offered a clear account of its principles: 'The Cubist poem is not guided in its development by the working out of the story line.' It is rather a 'superimposed succession of

---

bunuel/entrevistas/bardem.htm (accessed 3 April 2017). The date given, however, cannot be considered authoritative. The Lorca in the photograph is identical to a 1922 portrait of Lorca with García Maroto, which is reproduced and discussed in Juan Manuel Bonet, 'Quince instantáneas lorquianas (y una coda postumista) in *Teoría del duende*, ed. Enrique Juncosa (Granada: Centro Fundación Federico García Lorca, 2015), 83–120 (90–93).

21   In a letter to his good friend Melchor Fernandez Almagro dated 17 February 1922 and posted from Granada, where Lorca was finishing his degree, the poet confesses that he feels very alienated from the literary atmosphere of 'poetic decay' [descomposición poética] in the nation's capital (*E* 143). Spanish *Ultra* was breaking up around then. And Lorca was discovering the world of flamenco. On Spain's 'rich oral life' in the *tertulias* see the discussion in Roberta Quance, 'Espacios masculinos/femeninos: Norah Borges en la vanguardia', *Dossiers feministes* [Valencia], 10 (2007), 233–48.

22   Ian Gibson, *Lorca y el mundo gay. 'Caballo azul de mi locura'* (Barcelona; Planeta, 2009), 112.

23   See the diptych 'Diurnal' in the Appendix to this volume. In one of his letters (August 1923) Lorca jokes that the *ultraístas* had mistreated the shepherdess Amarilis because they were so taken with the 'Eva porvenirista [futuristic Eve]' (*E* 198).

notes and reflections without a causal link'.[24] By 1925 Torre, on the basis of 'El Libro de las Suites', a book that was yet to appear, would claim Lorca as 'the best poet akin to *ultraísmo*'.[25]

Around 1 May 1921 Lorca assures his family that he is, on Juan Ramón Jiménez's advice, going to self-publish and that he will bring out two books, one a collection of older work (which is in fact the *Libro de poemas*, 1921) and the other

> ...a book that I have composed here [Madrid] of extraordinarily new things in the form of 'Suites', which I think is the most perfect stuff I have produced.
>
> This second book has the advantage of being the most advanced work yet that is being done in poetry and it balances out my first work as a poet, which is on the other hand interesting and sincere. (*E* 114)

Yet Lorca is also hopeful that his friend Gregorio Martínez Sierra will help him publish in a new collection he will launch in the autumn (*E* 117).

As the summer proceeds, Lorca's collection of 'advanced work' grows, so that by early August 1921 he begins to speak optimistically, again, of a new volume of poetry, as he tells a friend:

> Now I am resting in this wonderful country and I am hard at work on a dramatic poem and my poetry in a new mould, a new aesthetic. (*E* 127)[26]

He insists to his friend Adolfo Salazar that what he is working on is the best poetry he has written so far:

> ...for I am pinning all my hopes on what I am doing now, because it seems like the best and finest work I have yet produced, so that it can be brought out in the autumn.
>
> I am working hard and I think you will like what I am doing, because I think it's better than the *suites* you already know. Do you want me to send you something? I call these things 'songs with a reflection' because I want only that: to give the sublime sensation of reflection with my words, removing anything 'salomonic' from their trembling. (*E* 122)

---

24   Torre's article, 'Los poetas cubistas franceses' appeared in *Cosmópolis*, 12, no. 36 (1921), 603–28 (p. 606). The article was incorporated into his *Literaturas europeas de vanguardia* (1925; Seville: Renacimiento-Biblioteca del Rescate).

25   Guillermo de Torre, *Literaturas europeas de vanguardia*, 107.

26   What might it have contained? Maurer offers a tentative list in *E* 123–24, noting that thirteen had been composed in July and at least three more in August, making sixteen altogether. The 'dramatic poem' Lorca mentions has not been identified.

Lorca's concern to remove anything 'salomónico' in his verse has been taken to mean anything decorative or rhetorical.[27] It is a reasonable conjecture, since the term refers to the volutes that differentiate an Ionic capital from a Doric one. Yet there is another way to think of this. For, although the poet seeks clarity and simplicity, the object of his editing pencil is a 'trembling' that he wants both to preserve and control: 'trembling' (or quivering, quaking) is the quality of what is new and alive (see 'Song of the Motionless Gardener'), and this original freshness should not be allowed to dry up. But it is also an effect, perhaps, of what is reflected in water – the temporal, running nature of verse – and is therefore hard to pin down with precision.

As we know, the volume did not materialize, and by January 1922 Lorca is still talking about revisions: 'I finished putting the final touches on the *suites…*' (*E* 136). However, he is also unexpectedly happy with other writing that he has been doing. What initially must have seemed an exile from the city has given him a new perspective on what he has in his own back yard, so to speak. For Lorca had finally bowed to his father's demand that he return to Granada to finish his university degree, and there he will spend some twenty months, from the summer of 1921 to February 1923. Under the intellectual guidance of Manuel de Falla, he had discovered the world of *cante jondo* [deep song, flamenco] and produced a draft of what would eventually be his *Poema del cante jondo*. Although its inspiration is traditional, he tells a friend back in Madrid, slipping briefly into the avant-garde idiom, that he has written an 'American *puzzle*' (*E* 137). Perhaps that is because its compositions are constructed along the lines of a *suite* – in pieces – and involve a reader's performance and decoding of fragmented narrative.[28]

The summer of 1922 sees Lorca writing more *suites* (such as *Madrigals*), but a latent problem surfaces. In a letter of uncertain date, perhaps September of 1922, according to the editor, Lorca confides to a friend that he is dissatisfied with his inner world:

> I am living a hand-me-down life. [*Vivo de prestado.*] What I have inside does not belong to me. My soul is absolutely unopened. [...] In short, dear Regino, I am unhappy now and bored with my artificial inner world. (*E* 158)

---

27   Luis García Montero, *El lector llamado Federico García Lorca* (Madrid: Taurus, 2016), 183.

28   See Roberta Ann Quance, *In the Light of Contradiction: Desire in the Poetry of Federico García Lorca* (Oxford: Legenda, 2010), 137–62.

The letter marks a crisis of self-representation, when the poet thinks that of the 'thousand Federicos' that he has seen 'lying in the attic of the past' and the thousand that in the future will 'fly off without direction' like so many balloons – not one is really him. It is not surprising, then, that he worries aloud: 'I am terrified of publishing', he says (*E* 160).

And so, the book of *suites* did not surface in the autumn of 1922; and the new year of 1923 sees Lorca a bit on the defensive about what to do with his unpublished work.[29] The last firm news we have about the composition of *suites* relates to what is certainly the most ambitious one, and also the most enigmatic, since Lorca left no outline for it. In July 1923 he reports that he has finished the long poem *In the Garden of the Lunar Grapefruits*, although he also says that he is willing to work all summer to perfect it (*E* 196). Some two weeks later, in a second letter, he is ready to share what he considers finished enough (*E* 205), while at the same time lamenting that he must release the *suites*: 'I suffer more and more with every passing day to see that I must publish my *suites* right away' (*E* 200).[30] The poems were 'Pórtico [Portico], 'El sátiro blanco' [The White Satyr], 'Arco de lunas' [Moonbow], 'Canción del muchacho de siete corazones' [Song of the Seven-Hearted Boy], 'Otra estampita [Another Little Picture], 'Tierra Cielo' [Earth Sky], 'Cancioncilla del niño que no nació [Little Ditty of the Unborn Child], and 'Amanecer y repique' [Dawn and Pealing Bells]. As Lorca describes the 'poem' at this point, we can see that it is conceived as a narrative, with a beginning, middle, and end. But only eight individual poems are reproduced and the entire *suite* has been reconstructed to include approximately twenty poems. From what Lorca says in his second letter, we may infer that the other poems in the *suite* existed in draft but that they were not quite finished to his satisfaction. And these would include, presumably, such important pieces as 'Perspective', 'Garden', 'Encounter', 'Song of the Motionless Gardener' or 'White Scent', poems that develop the theme of seeds, untaken paths, and a complex metaphysical view of love. What we do see from the poems he offered his friend José Ciria is that unrequited love is on his mind – 'Another Little Picture' features 'unloved maidens' – and that he has chosen to give a voice and presence to the unborn children who 'pursue' him.

---

29   See *E* 176; a letter to his family in February 1923 alludes to 'a lack of understanding on Father's part'.

30   Note that Lorca des not refer to his 'poem' as a *suite*, although it has been considered as such by editors. Could it be the 'dramatic poem' he had begun in the late summer of 1921, mentioned in his correspondence (*E* 127)?

Aesthetically he is convinced that this 'poem' is a thing apart. He believes that it is 'motionless' and that this is a desideratum. He did not want these poems to have 'ritmo' [rhythm] or 'viento' [wind] – but, I would suggest, to seem like a series of moments in a vision:

> The landscapes in this poem are absolutely motionless, without any wind or rhythm at all. I saw how my verse slipped from my hands, how my poetry fled from me and was *alive*. As a reaction to that feeling, my poem right now is ecstatic and sonambulant. My *garden* is the garden of possibilities, the garden of what is not but what could (and at times) should have been, the garden of theories that went by unnoticed and of children who were not born. Every word in the poem was a butterfly and I had to catch each of them, one by one. (*E* 196–97)

The reader is told that the vision proceeds from the land of the unliving (that which has no being in the present world) and so past and future are collapsed, and almost all the anchors of narrative are gone. The *suite* records 'theories' [processions of images] that are vouchsafed the traveller on his night journey before he returns to earth at dawn, and they exist without him, independently, in a different world.

The prospect of publishing a collection of *suites* (with, perhaps, some songs) weighs on the poet's mind but, despite at least two more approaches in late 1923, no volume materialized. If Lorca had a collection of *suites* nearly finished by the end of the summer, it was but one more 'unborn' version of a work that was to experience further deferral.[31] He knew very well that his failure to publish was going to fuel the legend growing up around him that he was an oral poet, a kind of latter-day *jongleur*, who did not feel comfortable with the 'finality' of the printed word.[32] Perhaps he did not feel

---

31 Interestingly, he specifies that he has not given *all* of his *suites* for publication (*E* 215). Lorca apparently envisaged a small anthology of *suites* and songs for the series *Cuadernos Literarios*, prepared by Alfonso Reyes, Enrique Díez-Canedo and José Moreno Villa. See the editorial note in *E* 215. On the attempts and offers to publish the *suites* see Melissa Dinverno, *Listening Through Mirrors: Representing García Lorca's Suites* (unpublished doctoral dissertation, University of Michigan, 2000), 66–78 and a summary in Quance, *In the Light of Contradiction*, 167–69.

32 Indeed, poet and critic Gerardo Diego would refer to him as a 'juglar' in a review of *Canciones* upon its release in 1927. See the reprinted text in *FGL, Boletín de la Fundación Federico García Lorca*, No. 2 (December 1987), 42–45 (p. 42). On this topic see the perceptive article by Beverly de Long-Tonelli, 'In the Beginning Was the End: Lorca's New York Poetry', *Anales de la literatura española contemporánea*, 12 (1987), 243–57. However, the experience with the *suites* suggests is that it is in these crucial early years that Lorca's

satisfied aesthetically with some of his work (as his exasperation in 1922 suggests). But there is little room to think that he disavowed his project. In his last known interview Lorca mentions the unpublished project by name, *Suites*, 'a book on old themes that I have put a lot of love and work into'.[33]

According to Melissa Dinverno, the very concept of a *suite* implied a certain mobility, in that it could be taken apart or rearranged.[34] In effect, around 1926 Lorca made a very serious revision. By Dinverno's count, he moved as many as thirty-five poems from the *suites* into the book he would title *Canciones*, and at the same time he made plans to bring out not one but three unpublished works, which he happily envisaged as a 'set' and in which he saw 'an odd unity' (*E* 329). Lorca was bent on waving away once and for all the legend that he was an oral poet. Had he been successful we would probably consider *Suites*, *Poema del cante jondo* [Poem of the Deep Song] and *Canciones* [Songs] a poetic cycle in its own right. Even though, as Dinverno has noted, the book of *suites* might then have been a very reduced affair.[35]

Given that Lorca tried at several points to publish his *suites*, in some form, we may have to accept, as Dinverno has suggested, that his project had a shifting identity. Each time it was tackled for publication, its contents would have altered: grown or been pruned under Lorca's critical eye. As the years wore on, as poetic fashion changed (surrealism would soon come into the picture) and social realities grew more pressing, the poet would no doubt have been stricter and stricter about what he was willing to stand over in print, just as he might have had misgivings about what his truth was and how much of a younger self he wished to leave on view.[36] Certainly, in some of his personal correspondence Lorca suggests that he has learned not to leave some aspects of himself open for prying eyes:'there are certain

hesitations about publishing become a legend.

33 Antonio Otero Seco, 'Una conversación inédita con Federico García Lorca. Índice de las obras inéditas que dejó el gran poeta', in *OC* III, 625–27.

34 Dinverno, *Listening*, 99 and 'García Lorca's Suites', 311: '…the text of a *suite* is structurally founded on motion'.

35 Melissa Dinverno, 'García Lorca's Suites', 320 and also *Listening Through Mirrors*, which delves more deeply into the question of possible versions of a book of *suites*. For discussion of the three books as a cycle and how they interrelate see Quance, *In the Light of Contradiction.*

36 Note the apologetic way the editor refers to the *Primeras canciones*, a miscellaneous volume published in 1936, which includes some early *suites*: 'Las *Primeras Canciones* (1922) pertenecen a un libro de adolescencia aún no ordenado por su autor' [First Songs (1922) belongs to a book of adolescence still unarranged by its author].

sentiments that one must not show ... and I know a thing or two about this! (truly)' (*E* 241).[37] The *suites* as Lorca might have wanted them to appear in a book – and with the kind of reception he might have wished – remained a work in progress, of a promissory nature. I have tried to preserve their *promising* quality by including as many as I thought translated reasonably well, even if some are uneven or unfinished.[38]

Although the French scholar André Belamich gathered Lorca's manuscripts en masse into a posthumous volume (having translated them into French in 1981 for the Pléiade edition), the *suites* have been relatively ignored for nearly twenty years. And only recently has interest in them quickened. The manuscripts deposited in the Fundación Federico García Lorca, are dense with a variety of textual problems, some of which not only make individual poems hard to finalize but even call into question which poems were finally intended for a specific sequence. But these and other problems which editors have detailed, should not be allowed to detract from a body of work that enriches our understanding of García Lorca's early lyric cycle and offers important clues to other major works.

Beyond the conviction that he was doing something new, how did Lorca think of his work? His first metaphor for the verse he was writing can be interpreted in various ways, as a comment on form, on at least some of the content and even, perhaps, as a way to read them. As we have seen, he described the *suites* in 1921 as 'songs with a reflection'. This has been taken by at least one critic as an allusion to content, to poems that talk about mirrors, echoes, reverberations of all kinds, and by extension to the existence of different perspectives on a subject.[39] It may also refer to the way in which a great many of the poems engage with the idea of a reflected self, through allusion to the mirrors and bodies of water that return his gaze.[40]

37 Lorca's complaint to Melchor Fernández Almagro comes at the close of his confession about the strange and perhaps curative effect the sea has on him: 'Standing before the sea, I forget my sex, my identity [mi condición], my soul, my gift for tears ... everything!'

38 Of the *suites* translated in Lorca's *Complete Poems* I have not included *Palmeras, Newton, Cuco-cuco-cucó, Seis canciones de anochecer, Ruedas de fortuna, Momentos de la tarde, Epitafio de un pájaro, [Suite], Meditaciones y alegorías del agua*. See Maurer's edition of *Collected Poems* for translations of these *suites* (by Jerome Rothenberg).

39 See Candelas Gala, *Poetry, Physics, and Painting in Twentieth-Century Spain* (Basingstoke, Hampshire: Palgrave Macmillan, 2011).

40 This leads to the subject of Narcissus, which emerges more prominently in *Canciones*. Dinverno, however, has pieced together one *suite* on the subject which she argues was suppressed by the poet because of other connotations given Narcissus (same-sex love and desire). See *Listening Through Mirrors*, 228–43.

But Lorca may even have thought of the poetic form itself as a mirror, as a letter to Melchor Fernández Almagro from October 1923 (*E* 212) suggests, for here Lorca refers to excerpts of *The Return*, a *suite* that is indebted to Galician-Portuguese lyric, as 'little mirrors' (*espejillos*). It is, I would suggest, the peculiar pattern of repetitions in his poem that can be seen as reflecting mirrors.

For André Belamich the *suites* mirror most poignantly the poet's disappointed desire and his thwarted hopes to become a father, a theme that Belamich summed up as having to do with 'seeds that never flowered', and which he links to some of the masterpieces of Lorca's theatre. As we shall see, this view takes its inspiration primarily in the last *suite*. For Charles Marcilly the *suites* are chiefly metaphysical and have to do with unanswerable questions about the beginnings and ends of individual life and the laws of nature. Candelas Gala, on the other hand, contends that these poems should be read in light of the scientific principles underlying cubism, and so she explores the analogies they present with some of the most advanced physics of Lorca's day. For Federico Bonaddio, the *suites* represent a moment of transition, when the self-consciously sincere lyrical subject of the *Libro de poemas* – Lorca's first book of verse – is under pressure to remove himself from the poem and to turn his back on sentimentality. For all that the self remains at the centre, as we shall see, in the *suites* perception and emotion are not necessarily ascribed to an I that is anything more than a particular enunciative stance.[41]

Hegel had defined the lyric as the most subjective of genres, but lyricism and inwardness in all forms had come under attack by the futurists and never regained credibility.[42] In the postwar years the Hispanic avant-garde engaged in polemic about the place of the I in poetry. How should the poet's I be reflected in his or her poem? In at least two of the little magazines that Lorca would have known and probably read we find critics weighing the virtues of new writing that avoided the I altogether. For César Arroyo, the editor

---

41   See Candelas Gala, *Poetry, Physics and Painting*, 180–83. Gala takes Lorca's remark that he is working on 'canciones con reflejo' to refer to all of the *suites* and builds a provocative argument about the perspectivism in the poet's world view, informed by analogies with new developments in physics. There is a different emphasis in Federico Bonaddio, *Federico García Lorca. The Poetics of Self-Consciousness*, London: Tamesis, 2010. Bonaddio's analysis of the early *Libro de poemas* charts the different concepts of the poet which are being discarded in the *suites*: the poet as an interpreter of nature, the poet as a seer.

42   See Jonathan Culler, *Theory of the Lyric* (Cambridge, Mass: Harvard University Press, 2015), 94. 104–109 for discussion.

of *Cervantes*, the absence of the I in haiku dissolved the difference between
writerly and readerly perception entirely. In *Cosmópolis* the young Jorge
Luis Borges applauded his compatriot Macedonio Fernández for writing as
if the I did not exist, an idea which he would go on to develop once he was
back home in Buenos Aires.[43] Although Lorca did not pronounce himself
upon the subject critically, he left one early *suite* – titled *I [I]* – in which
he jokes that he is crucified by the pronoun.

Federico Bonaddio speaks usefully of the 'I's reconfiguration' in the *suites*
(and *canciones*). Even if the I is not the centre of attention, we should not
forget that the poetry is lyric; it is filtered through a particular subjectivity and
even more particularly through the heart.[44] Consider, too, that if reflections
of all kinds are found in the *suites*, one is compelled to mark the weight
of the poet's conviction that his heart has found none: it is 'without echo'
('World', *Countries*), and it 'sails over the girls / at the fair'. The lyric
subject is buffeted by the winds of desire and a pessimism about love that is
unmistakable. As we shall see, his trials eventually include the questioning
of sexual identity.

In what follows I propose to look at some of the reiterated imagery and
phrasing in the *suites* in the hope of bringing to light an intricate textual
constellation.

The colour of a counterworld

If *Blue River* from late 1920 is among the first of Lorca's *suites*, it is also
the sequence that contains an important element in Lorca's imagination,
bringing sky and water together in the colour that Rubén Darío made famous
with his *Azul* (1888) and before him Mallarmé, with his appeal to *l'azur*.
Lorca develops the idea in connection with a poetic sanctuary where he
will find disappointments compensated in part, through the very act of
writing. The image returns in *Secrets* and in *Water Suite*. To follow a 'blue
road' involves leaving behind the 'love of my nighttime hours' – whether
that love is real or only imagined. Proclaiming himself the 'tamer' – or
circus-trainer (*domador*) – of 'ominous butterflies', the lyrical subject looks
beyond erotic love:

---

43   Jorge Luis Borges, 'La lírica argentina contemporánea. Selección y notas', *Cosmópolis*.
1, no. 38 (1921), 640–51. The reference is from p. 641. César Arroyo's remarks appear in
'La nueva poesía en América', *Cervantes* (August 1919), 105–13.
44   Thus Bonaddio notes shrewdly (*The Poetics*, 13) that an invisible heart is visible in
'Conjuro' from the *Poema del cante jondo*, thanks to the poet-conjurer's sleight-of-hand.

Down the blue path
I go,
a tamer of
sombre stars,
until the Universe
fits inside my heart.

To take 'the blue path' is, in the end, to comprehend the universe and to abandon a love that for now is both secret and more limited. A journey of 'a thousand years' is needed – as if to say that he must be reborn (in a different time and place).

A blue world is a counterworld, wherein lies the ideal. But it is also – or at least, it becomes – the colour that is associated with the moon, the nocturnal and a world offering a counterpoint to the sun, fertility, and a heterosexual economy. As such it can connote what may not come to be or what must be guarded, including poetry itself, as we see in a poem that was discarded from *Moments of Song* 'Canción muerta' [Dead Song]: 'Mi azul canción ha muerto / antes de nacer' [My blue song has died / before it was born]. Another lyric included here in an Appendix ('Mown Field'), as perhaps a broken-off fragment of the last *suite*, develops the lyrical subject's complex relation to such a world. For while the seeds 'dream' of fruition in a diurnal regime, the lyrical subject's soul is identified with the impossible fruit that has been transformed under the light of the moon – the blue sheaf of wheat and the white poppy. I will come back to this in detail in the context of notes on translation.

The 'bitter garden of questions' (*Herbals*, *In the Garden…*)

Throughout the *suites* but especially in the last *suite*, with its bifurcation into two sites – garden and forest – Lorca reworks traditional metaphor to designate the space of literary exploration. Reaching back as far as Plato, who spoke in the *Phaedrus* of a garden of letters, the garden is a time-honoured metaphor in the Renaissance for a poetic collection. It is also, at least, since medieval lyric, a space where lovers meet. Lorca uses the metaphor in an intimate vein, somewhat like Juan Ramón Jiménez, to talk about the verbal space of one's dreams and emotions. But he adds a sharply different perspective when he recognizes that the garden of love is a place where the poetic subject is confronted with painful matters. (One cannot help thinking here of some of the dramatic possibilities in the setting that

Lorca will exploit in works like *The Love of Don Perlimplín with Belisa in the Garden*, where the garden is like Gethsemane for his Christ-like hero, or *Doña Rosita the Spinster*, the unwed rose in her garden. It is no accident that the origins of these plays go back to 1923 and 1924, respectively.) A 'bitter garden' of questions crops up in a poem from the *suite Ruedas de Fortuna* (*Wheels of Fortune*), while in *Herbals*, the young man who is in dialogue with time's travelling salesman intuits that what lies ahead of him is a 'garden of bitter fruit'.[45] The logic behind this imagery surfaces in the final *suite* and oddly enough in the early draft version, *In the Wood*, where the narrator is vouchsafed a vision: 'Soul, crippled but crystal-clear, / behold your garden! // The old full moons / shone against the leaves on the trees / like immense crystal disks'. Lorca's narrator had announced earlier that he was going to the 'unassailable wood / of lunar grapefruits'. That is to say, he aimed to find his way *through* a wood *to* a garden; yet this one does not grow the oranges – the sweet fruit – associated with marriage between a man and a woman (as in the old world view of traditional lyric). Indeed, the 'crystal disks' might be the emblems of failed romance, of no fruitful sentiment at all. Nonetheless, they are a beautiful vision of the moon's 'fruit', and one cannot help wondering if here – the only place we find an allusion to 'lunar grapefruits' (or oranges) – the poet has perhaps pointed diffidently to the idea that there can be beauty in a non-procreative love and desire.

Concentric circles and spirals; the straight line

It was Alan Trueblood who first called attention to this important element in Lorca's early verse: a series of objects, natural or man-made, are evoked through simple geometric forms.[46] A rose, rippling water, a spiral, a Corinthian column. In the context of love, circles arise in connection with the traditional rose of (heterosexual) love and passion or the symbol of the ring and commitment (as in 'Glorieta'), but they also appear in the context of frustrated movement, the inability to advance. In *Madrigals* the poetic speaker evokes a lover's embrace as an imprisonment: the lover's words reverberate in his heart (like a stone flung into the water), but he is not free to move ahead: 'I am a prisoner / of your concentric circles.' That the circle contrasts with the

---

45   See *OC* I, 297.
46   Alan Trueblood, 'Imágenes geométricas en la poesía temprana de Lorca', en *La voluntad de humanismo. Homenaje a Juan Marichal*, eds Birute Ciplijauskaité and Christopher Maurer (Barcelona: Anthropos, 1990), 233–47.

straight line is apparent. This for Trueblood is an aesthetic choice and one which Octavio Paz once glossed as the formal archetypes of either narrative or poetry.[47] But it becomes apparent, too, that there are values attached to each form which have a certain inflection for gender. An unsatisfactory choice is posed in 'Spiral' (*Snail*): 'Oh arrow-straight line! / Lance without a knight. / How my meandering [salomónica] path / dreams of your light!' To be straight and forthright in pursuing one's goal is to be like a knight; to go in a scroll-like path (like the snail inside its shell) is to be introspective and hesitant, both of which, traditionally, are undesirable qualities for the male in the sphere of heterosexual romance.[48] Thus, one scholar, who has analysed *Snail*, has called attention to the subtlety of the spiral image in the context of the poet's lament that he is unable to release a child 'from his heart' – which is to say, become a father, whether of a child or of a younger self ('Ballad of the White Snail).[49]

The heart like a bullseye

A number of the *suites* point again and again to the heart, though often in an ironic way (which makes them something of an exception in Lorca's verse). Lorca is hard put to defend love and emotion in the face of the avant-garde's assault on sentimentality. But we can see his divided loyalties. In 'World' (*Countries*) the poet, addressing his solitary 'heart without echo', claims that 'the universe begins and ends / in you'. In 'Sesame' (*Moments of Song*), where reality and reflection are one and the same – indistinguishable, perhaps – a loving desire is an absolute: 'Nothing here but one heart / and one wind'. And yet experience intrudes painfully on this metaphysics. In 'Summit' (*Shadow*) the heart (like Saint Sebastian) is an unhappy target for Cupid's arrow: 'When I get to the mountaintop // (Oh desolate heart / Saint Cupid Sebastian)' and in still another, 'Street Fair' (*Fairs*), the poet marvels that he can await the torment of love with delight: 'This heart of mine, / revelling in pain, flung open / for the arrow!' Indulging in self-mockery, the voice in 'Ruby Disk' sounds like a barker or a carny (*Castle of Fireworks*)

---

47   Octavio Paz, *El arco y la lira* (México: Fondo de Cultura Económica, 1957), 69.
48   Maurer (*E* 156) has noted how important the imagery is in some of the poems written in 1922: *Riverside Reveries*; *Madrigals*. It also crops up in a projected book *Meditations and Allegories of the Water* (*CP* 348) and in the prologue to the last *suite* in its Garden version.
49   Giovanni Caravaggi, 'Struttura e poesia di una "diferencia" lorchiana: la Suite del Caracol', in *L'impossibile/possibile di Federico García Lorca*, Atti del convegno di studi, Salerno, 9–10 maggio 1988 (Naples: Pubblicazioni degli Studi di Salerno/Edizioni Scientfiche Italiani, 1989), 59–75.

inviting the object of desire or the spectator to marvel at a circus act: 'All arrows / to this round / heart // All eyes / on this round / heart.'[50]

The poetic motif eventually leads us to one of Lorca's abstract pen and ink drawings titled 'Saint Sebastian' and allows us to venture the interpretation that the drawing from 1927 masks the suffering of love. In the middle of his affair with Salvador Dali and the aesthetic exchange between the two, which was focused on the saint, Lorca suggests that the face which is discernible at the centre of his drawing – a minimalist representation consisting of one cognizant eye, an orifice for the mouth, and six converging arrows – stands in for his heart.[51]

Language

In some of the earliest poems such as 'Capriccios' Lorca plays with language, as he reflects on the arbitrary and yet seemingly binding relation between the signifier and the signified. This is one place where we can see best how he might have been influenced by Ramón Gómez de la Serna, Madrid's earliest avant-gardist. In the *tertulia* Ramón led at the Antigua Botillería y Café de Pombo, on the Calle Carretas near the Plaza del Sol, the young Lorca might have heard many examples of his *greguerías*, aphorisms dense with humorous metaphors. Ramón devised an alphabet of such *greguerías*:[52]

> The T is the hammer of the alphabet. […] The Y is the champagne glass…

Ramón played with the visual image of letters, much as we see Lorca doing in the *suite* entitled 'I' [*Yo*], where he claims that the letter Y is 'the winnowing fork of academics' or in the last *suite* in the vivid image of question marks as 'sickles of interrogation'. He can even experiment with embedding an

---

50   The barker speaks also in 'Pregón' [Barker's Cry], a poem that was included in the Appendix to *Canciones*. The poetic subject's suffering is treated like a circus act. See *Canciones y Primeras canciones*, ed. Piero Menarini (Madrid: Espasa Calpe-Clásicos Castellanos, 1986), 310. Significantly, the motifs of the garden (of disillusionment) and of the concentric circle also figure there.

51   Lorca's drawing (CAT 130) is reproduced in his *Libro de los dibujos de Federico García Lorca*, ed. by Mario Hernández (Madrid: Tabapress and the Fundación Federico García Lorca, 1990). Dali's text 'San Sebastián', which was dedicated to Lorca, appeared in the poet's little magazine *gallo* (No. 1, February 1928), 1–12, as a manifesto in favour of a kind of cool, rational aesthetic that would be the opposite of putrefaction, the avantgardists' term for art based on the contagion of sentiment.

52   Ramón's first collection was *Greguerías* (Prometeo: Valencia, 1918). I have quoted from his *Total de greguerías*, 2nd edn (Madrid: Aguilar, 1962), 173 and 175, respectively.

acrostic in one of his *Capriccios* ('Tree'). On the whole, however, Lorca was not much seduced by Apollinaire's famous call for a 'visual lyricism' like the variety exemplified in his *caligrammes* or the avant-garde's experiments in typography and visual arrangement on the page.[53]

The poet's insistence that the signifier *sol* can replace the referent is an insight into the illusion without which the ordinary, everyday function of language would be all but impossible: the idea that all of the signifiers in a language are necessarily the way they are. Years before Saussure and his *Cours de linguistique générale* (1913) came to writers' attention, stressing the arbitrary nature of the sign, we have what many would term the modern poet's view of language's signifiers: the conviction that words become natural objects.

Childhood and childhood amusements

Several of the *suites* centre on childhood, its amusements as well as its fears or the regrets it awakens in the adult, whose voice is the one through which the child's perspective is filtered. Given that the older poet is the gateway for the reader's access to the child, it is probably not surprising that some very adult concerns colour the retrospective gaze. In *The Return* the poet associates childhood with a time when he had 'wings', and the desire to return is acute inasmuch as every passing minute reminds him that he is losing more and more of a treasure that cannot be replenished. To go back to yesterday is to reclaim the dawn (*amanecer*) and a full potential that dwindles over the years. The poet knows that being in time moves him ever closer to death. The only resolution is in paradox: 'I want to die while I am / yesterday'. The enjambment brings out the paradox that it is only in this imagined return (which will cancel forward movement) that he has real being (and perhaps, by extension, only in the poem, as well). A child's perspective is also the key to *The Forest of Clocks*, but here the return to childhood – which is triggered by the sound of a mechanical organ he once had – seems to force the poetic subject to face a test of his heart that he would rather not have to face: 'Through here! Through here!' This is not in the first instance a fear of death in the woods but a test that is the equivalent of facing death. Lorca chooses rather consistently in the *suites* to adopt a child's perspective to dramatize painful sentimental choices or disappointments.

---

53 See 'El espíritu nuevo y los poetas. Un estudio póstumo de Apollinaire', *Cosmópolis*, 1 (1919), 17–28.

Childhood appeared to offer a world of androgyny, before sexual roles were apportioned and one might feel the impossibility of complying with them. That is one way to read the final lines of the final poem in *The Garden of the Dark-Haired Girls*, in which both a male phallic symbol and the emblem of a young girl's virginity are wished away.

Sometimes it is only a phrase or an image that flashes forth, as we have already mentioned in connection with *Fairs*, to warn us that simple nostalgia for childhood play or innocence is not on the agenda. It comes as a bit of a jolt to see the heart, again, at the centre of these poems. It suggests that when the poet recalls childish amusements – the merry-go-round, the circus – it is to treat a very adult problem in a tongue-in-cheek way. We imagine the poetic subject in these texts as a young man poised between childhood and maturity, close enough to remember the excitement and promise of the fair and the *verbena* but removed enough to use them as a source of metaphors for his sentimental disappointments.

In the Madrid that Lorca became acquainted with in the late teens and early twenties, both the light-hearted side of childhood and its ignorance of the dark were being explored. There was, on the one hand, the avant-garde that revelled in the circus, in *verbenas* [street fairs] and amusement parks. Impossible not to think first of Ramón Gómez de la Serna and his popular book *El circo* [The Circus] (1917). But behind this one-man movement there was also an older generation of poets who supported the pedagogical reform of the Institución Libre de Enseñanza (founded in 1873), namely Juan Ramón Jiménez and Antonio Machado. Jiménez's *Platero and I* (1914) established the significance of autobiographical inquiry into childhood; Machado's poetry placed enormous importance on the fact that children's voices at play were often the subterranean channel that kept traditional song alive.[54] Although the influence of both is evident in the *suites*, Lorca's elder colleagues regard childhood as teachers of children would. In the *suites* Lorca regards it as a treasure that he has lost and yet, paradoxically, can draw upon to explore his most intimate concerns. Only later in *Poet in New York* or *Once Five Years Pass* does the poet frankly acknowledge the contradictory mixture of innocence and corruption that as an adult he finds in the child.

---

54   As in the well-known poem: 'Yo escucho los cantos / de viejas cadencias / que los niños cantan / cuando en coro juegan' from *Soledades* (1907) [I listen to the songs / of old cadences / that the children sing / when they play in a ring]. See Antonio Machado, *Poesía y prosa*, Vol. II; *Poesías completas* ed. Oreste Macri (Madrid: Espasa-Calpe/Fundación Antonio Machado, 1989), 433.

Voyages/Journeys

More than one *suite* sketches a rudimentary narrative, however brokenly, devoid as they are of explicit connectors, which would have raised objections among avant-gardists about the interference of an *anécdota* [storyline] with the purity of painting or lyric. *Blue River, The Forest of Clocks, Herbals* and *In the Garden* (or *Wood*) *of the Lunar Grapefruits* all involve a traveller into an otherworldly realm. He may be, respectively, a dissatisfied poet, a little boy lost, a space traveller, or the hero of a fairy-tale who sallies forth into the land of the unliving, yet he is always seeking self-knowledge and renewal of the sources of his poetry in a confrontation with his heart and his desire. What is undeniable is the air of secrecy in which the poet shrouds the hero of the last *suite*: the garden for which he is bound is walled in silence, and at the end, after meeting a woman with whom he might have had children ['Encounter'], the narrator imposes silence on himself. These are, however, two very different kinds of silence: one is hermetic, suggesting the silence of the mystical and ineffable, while the other speaks of the need to censor oneself in the waking world.[55] It is only in the night world behind the looking glass that the narrator is free to explore his difference. Same-sex desire was very much an object of taboo in Lorca's day, and when his narrator suggests that he has found wisdom at the end of his journey – the knowledge that in another world, or in another time, he might have taken a different path, or that his soul is both that of a boy and a girl, as hermetic doctrine teaches – the consolation sounds bittersweet.

On the other hand, if the walled garden is a kind of parallel reality – where the still-to-be realized exists with its own compelling force – an idea which Dinverno traces to Maeterlinck – then the world behind the looking glass is a place that can be visited and inhabited at least for a time (Maurer, *CP* 911). It may be seen, I would suggest, as a kind of foreworld or back of the world (*trasmundo*) pressing on the waking world as we know it. And it is a world that impinges on Lorca's dramas, in particular, as they shift the emphasis of personal frustration onto the plight of characters onstage.

---

55 Dinverno *(Listening)* emphasizes the idea of a 'revelatory space' in connection with silence, developing her argument around the idea of a 'submerged suite', *Narcissus*, which was eventually broken up and dispersed. See pp. 197 ff (esp. p. 211)

Opening up the text: notes on this translation

> My essential things come to me.
> Refrains of other refrains.
> > 'Otherwise' [De otro modo]
> > *Canciones* (1927)

When I made up my mind to translate Lorca's *suites* my first concern was to find a voice for the poet that would connect him to the modern European tradition and to a group of poets like H. D., Pound, Eliot and Williams, who were his contemporaries. As much as I admired Jerome Rothenberg, who had translated the *suites* for the *Collected Poems*, I thought that he had missed some nuances in the Spanish and that at times his Lorca spoke like a poet from the American West.[56] But mostly I was concerned that he had decontextualized the *suites* from the poetic that Lorca was developing there and in two other works, which formed an early cycle.[57]

That poetic had affinities with haiku and with the early avant-garde movement of imagism and the tendency to build up a composition through fragments in collage. These, of course, were the concerns of early modernism and in their most striking form they are a cosmopolitan development, suggesting a contemporary, urban voice that would be equally at home in London or New York, even though the subject matter might be the *vega* [lowlands] or the rivers of Andalusia.

In the *suites* Lorca is subject to two major influences on his writing. He is on the one hand composing verse that is brief and fragmented, and on the other hand he is beginning to see that the structure and themes of traditional Iberian folksong – which has survived in fragments – can give him, ironically, the modern edge he is seeking. Both tendencies were pointed out by Mario Hernández before the *suites* were edited for the first time as a distinct body of work.[58]

---

56   On the matter of voice, see for example, 'Song in Tears' [Tearful Song] (*CP* 205): 'In that place, / o sweet babe of the fountain'; or 'Out on the prairie my heart / went dancing' ('Song with Reflections', *CP* 201)); or 'You must skip to my loo, / my darling' ('Chaparral', *In the Forest of Clocks*, *CP* 267); or 'Field got no roads / & town got no roofs' ('Countries', *CP* 297), or 'I lug around rings' (*Madrigals*, II), *CP* 347).

57   For discussion of this and other matters concerning Lorca in American translation see Jonathan Mayhew, *Apocryphal Lorca* (Chicago: U of Chicago P, 2009).

58   See his introduction to *Primeras canciones. Seis poemas gallegos. Canciones populares* (Madrid: Alianza, 1981) and *Canciones 1921–1924* (Madrid: Alianza, 1982).

The folksongs he heard while growing up had been polished like precious stones over the centuries, and the ones that proved most influential on the poetic diction of Lorca and other poets were the versions collected in songbooks by musicians and poets with a courtly, educated taste. In 1890 Francisco Asenjo Barbieri brought out his *Cancionero musical español de los siglos XV y XVI*, a collection that opened up a new world for an entire generation of poets. But Lorca also had firsthand experience: in January 1921 at the Residencia Lorca introduced his companions to folksongs from Granada which he himself had collected *(E* 97.) By the time he delivered his talk on the *cante jondo* in 1922 in Granada, he cited the work of distinguished folklorists such as the Catalan Felipe Pedrell who had gone before him.[59] Anyone who has read this lyric – whose corpus is uniquely rich – knows that while it is dense with nature symbolism it is also highly allusive and elegant. I wanted to give Lorca a voice that would reflect this tradition in its cultivated dimension, which is how Lorca's generation carried it on, as heirs of the work of poets like Lope de Vega and Luis de Góngora. This does not mean that I have given him a classic language, without regard to the different codes and registers in his early lyric. The *suites* are laced with allusions to authors as different as Plato, Lewis Carroll, Juan Ramón Jiménez, Hans Christian Andersen, and Maurice Maeterlinck; the language in which the poet speaks must be equally at home with philosophy and Greek myth as well as with the echoes of fairytale and folksong.

This particular project has convinced me more firmly than ever that the translator of poetry needs to have a good grasp of the poet's poetics (the way s/he conceives of poetry and builds a poem) as well as a working interpretation of the entire body of work of which the poem forms a part. Although I was translating only a portion of Lorca's oeuvre, I also wanted to be able to weigh my choices against the author's entire range. Ideally, the translator knows how the work at hand resonates both backwards and forwards in the rest of the poet's production. Part of this 'knowing' involves knowledge of how the poet's poetics evolve. The translation of the expressionistic, quasi surrealist *Poeta en Nueva York* will not pose the same challenges as the translation of the Gongorine ballads of the *Romancero gitano*. And when it comes to Lorca's early lyric – including his *Canciones*

---

59   In his lecture on the *cante jondo* from 1922 Lorca mentions [Felipe] Pedrell, Dámaso Ledesma, Eduardo Torner and *Olmeda*. See Marco Antonio de la Ossa Martínez (2014), García Lorca: la música y las canciones populares españolas', *Alpha (Osorno)*, (39), 93–121. https://dx.doi.org/10.4067/S0718-22012014000200008.

and the *Poema del cante jondo* – the translator will be faced with an urgent need to ponder the poet's debt to the techniques and themes of popular lyric.

This is not the place to attempt a 'finished' interpretation of any compilation of Lorca's *suites* – for all the reasons outlined earlier. But as I picked my way through these texts, I was reminded of some of the hermeneutical principles that come into play as we seek to interpret a work and I weighed the need, as a consequence, to translate in a way (sometimes falling shy of repetition) that would point to semantic complexes that could in turn lead to an interpretation. For example, the phrase '(Tarde descarriada)' from 'Canción sin abrir' [Unopened Song] (*CP* 202), is echoed in 'Torre' [Tower], a poem from the last *suite*, in the phrase 'pobre luz descarriada' ('poor misguided light') and again in 'Perspectiva' in reference to 'misguided' flowers in an other-worldly garden (Dinverno 276). Is a moral connotation always called for, or is the first poem an example of a desired ambiguity, of aimlessness? The *suites* are reticent, as Melissa Dinverno has said, yet we are in a position to say that a great deal of their reticence turns on matters of the heart or on desire and its unfulfillment. Eventually, I found that an argument could be made for the centrality of two terms that traversed the poems and which gathered meaning around them magnetically: the word *seed*, or the word *mirror*, or *looking-glass*, both of which may in Lorca's world be opened or closed. Taken together they seem to hint at all that the poet hoped for, both in terms of a poetic renewal as well as a more elusive personal one.

Let's look closely at how a translation might proceed that aimed to take into account both poetics and interpretation. The following is my translation of a poem that seems to have broken off from the last *suite*, which has been so difficult for editors to piece together:

> Mown field,
> the moonlight dissolving.
>
> Seeds' dreams
> go up in the air.
>
> A blue ear of grain,
> a white poppy.
>
> My soul,
> the only delirious
> flower.

Mown field,
the moonlight dissolving.

Lorca used a pattern found in Spanish Renaissance songbooks dating from the end of the 15th century which gathered traditional (oral) poetry for the first time. After presenting a refrain (*estribillo*), which would consist of a line or two drawn from oral tradition, Renaissance poets went on to develop a series of lines of their own invention that glossed and expanded on the refrain. Lorca imitates this practice but produces a poem that is in its entirety of his own invention, so that it has the *appearance* of traditionality.

The issue here for the translator is to retain the structure of the borrowed form (refrain and gloss) – knowing full well that there is no equivalent for it in English – and to weigh the significance of the early form's key features: the parallelisms that characterize it, ranging from syntactical to semantic to phonological in type. Here is Lorca's original Spanish:

El campo segado
y la luna disuelta.

Por el aire van los sueños
de las semillas.

Espiga azul
y amapola blanca.

Mi alma,
una sola flor
delirante.

El campo segado
y la luna disuelta.
              (*OC* I, 300–301)

In my translation, the question of preserving any phonological parallelisms is ruled out by the granite-like fact that all translators face: although we know that the sound of a poem shapes its sense, we have to leave that dimension behind. The sounds/signifiers of English and Spanish are different. One cannot, for example, preserve the alternation of a-o and e-a in the refrain, in the words *segado* and *disuelto*, if the meaning of the words is to be translated – though possibly an analogy could be built with other sounds. But syntactical parallelism is also broken in my translation, and perhaps it is not clear why. I might have said 'the field mown, / the moon dissolved' but I opted for a first line that placed the participle before the noun, like an ordinary adjective in English, and in the second line, moving further from the original, I avoided the past participle altogether and opted for a gerund.

Such are the issues facing a translator of poetry. What can we say of such choices here?

In part I wished instinctively to avoid the dull thud of an absolute phrase – (*now that*) the field (is) mown, (*now that*) the moon (is) dissolved – as if one were laying down a condition. I wanted to give the impression that the poet was setting a scene and throwing fragments at us with the sparing hand of the author of haiku. This is an avant-garde technique Lorca might have seen in oriental verse. And elsewhere I stressed this by substituting some conjugated verbs with gerunds, to make the impression captured more motionless.

What does it mean to say that the moon has 'dissolved'? It cannot be literal so we have to interpret figuratively. I think here of the visual effect created by a bright moon, when its soft light looks like thin, blue-white liquid poured over the land. And I had in the back of my mind a certain propensity in the *suites* for images that linked the moon with water, as in *Songs Beneath the Moon.*

I also reflected on the form of the traditional *villancico* (carol), a form that Lorca knew well and cultivated in *Songs* (1927). Beginning and ending with a refrain (an *estribillo*), a *villancico* was circular in form, according to some scholars, and drew a magic circle around itself where time and narrative did not encroach.[60] Although the gloss of the refrain often introduced a development, it did not move toward resolution. But did this mean that a *villancico* could not *move toward* such narrative, only to have its consequences denied or stalled? To me it seemed as if this modification of the traditional form to hint at narrative was a sign of Lorca's modernity.

I realized that Lorca's poem had acted powerfully on me because I read it almost cinematically, as if its refrain were leading us inside a frame. Its first two lines set a scene, and the rest developed a metaphorical event ('seeds' dreams / go up in the air'), which was perhaps a consequence of the harvest that had taken place. Instinctively, I preferred 'dissolving' to 'dissolved'; I wanted the poem to imply that the moon was still an active presence, as if we were dealing with a fade-in, and that this, together with the reapers who had done their job and gone, was causing the seeds' dreams of flowering

---

60   See Elizabeth Boretz, *Mysterious Realms. Functions of Imagery in Traditional Spanish Lyric and Balladry* (Newark, Delaware: Juan de la Cuesta, 1998), 52.

to disappear, as if they could melt before our eyes in a milky white field and something else might emerge. The colours blue and white suggested, mysteriously, that the ear of wheat (which was once yellow) and the poppy (once red) no longer existed as such but that by the light of the moon they were still present, if only as an ideal reality. The poem celebrates a different world view from that of the traditional lyric, while exploiting all of that lyric's symbols of fruition.

As a translator I have marvelled that a brief poem could be so complex. Lorca managed to perform this kind of feat many times in his early lyric. In this poem – possibly broken off from Lorca's last and most ambitious *suite, In the Garden of the Lunar Grapefruits* – we have a poetic in a nutshell, and I wanted to translate it in a way that would be consistent with an idea I had found running throughout the *suites* as a whole, beginning with his 'Blue River', in which the poem is posited as a counterworld, one that makes up for the disappointments of the real. To keep this 'blue road' ('Journey', *Secrets*) in sight, even if only just beneath the surface, was one of the touchstones of my work as a translator of the *suites.* I wanted to make sure that half-hidden meanings (in the secret mirrors that bounced back 'reflections') would not be impossible to catch sight of and that they would finally make sense and allow us to see a culmination in the last *suite*, where these concerns emerge most fully.

All writers are keenly aware of the different connotations of words. And translators must be as well, in both the source and target language. In a brief lyric sometimes a single word can alter our entire picture of who has given voice to the poem. In the suite *Secrets*, for example, I found that there were two ways to translate the phrase 'cazar luceros'. *Cazar* could be interpreted as either to hunt or to catch, depending upon what the quarry was: was it some sort of game animal or perhaps something collected, like butterflies? It remained to decide what kind of a hunter the poetic subject was and how the title 'Woodcutter' fit in. Were we perhaps talking about felling a tree so as to seize the stars entangled in its branches? I finally opted for 'hunt' to translate *cazar* because the remainder of the poem suggested that the poetic subject had 'bagged' and slung his prize over his shoulder.[61]

The word *remanso* required some flexibility. The scholar Ramón Menéndez Pidal had used the verb *remansarse* to talk about the way that the ballad form could include lyrical interludes that retarded the advance

---

61   And the image of 'bagging' game is repeated in 'Solitario', *Seis canciones de anochecer* [Six Songs at Nightfall] (*CP* 293).

of narrative.[62] A *remanso*, therefore, is not necessarily a 'backwater', with the negative connotation of stagnant water, but a place in the stream where there is pooling water or still water that invites reflection. Criticism has also stressed the significance of the contrast in Lorca's early lyric between a straight line and a 'salomonic' one (see the notes on *Madrigals*). I avoided the term 'salomonic' (sacrificing the glancing allusion to ambiguity in King Solomon's choice) and chose instead 'meandering' or 'spiralling', trusting that the title and the image of a spiralling conch shell might ferry Lorca's meaning across.

In '[Mown Field]' I had been confronted with the question of how to translate *segar* – whether to insist on the reaping of the wheat, which rings positively (making the Grim Reaper something of an oxymoron) – or to opt for the word 'mow', which has been put to use metaphorically throughout the history of English literature to speak of a life cut down before its time. I chose 'mown', because we do not think of a field strewn with wild grasses and flowers as being reaped. And in the poem I was convinced that we were not concentrating on the harvest but on a broken dream of a different fruition.

As I look over the finalized translations I see other issues that had to be resolved. One is enjambment and more generally the way syntax interacts with lineation in texts of *arte menor* (minor art), lines of fewer than nine syllables, like that found in folk metre. Thus the full stop in line 2 of the following from the *suite Water Jets* is counteracted by the placement of a new subject pronoun at the end of the line:

> Through the August air
> go the clouds. I
> dream I do not dream
> inside the fountain.[63]

The enjambment isolates the third line and the striking contradiction it contains. On more than one occasion I found myself using enjambment specifically to isolate lines on the page and thus to appeal to a visual reading of the poem. In this case there is also a subtle effect of somnambulism in the second line as the addition of I (*yo*) forces the reader not to let the voice fall at the completion of the sentence at the full stop.

---

62   See Ramón Menéndez Pidal, *Romancero hispánico* (Madrid: Espasa-Calpe, 1953), I, 60.
63   A *surtidor* is the jet of water shooting up from a basin that catches the water in a fountain. 'Fountain' comprehends both components but does not automatically stress the verticality of the water.

However, a different effect altogether is accomplished in *The Return*, when the poetic subject insists on throwing the gerund in line 4 into relief through enjambment. The translation has to make it clear that the poet is after a contradiction, so that 'Quiero morir siendo' is perceived as a viable wish in and of itself. My translation settles for something that is more of an explanation: 'I want to die while I am / dawn'. This is a way of implying that fulfilment in the past and the future is difficult to reach.

In some of the poems I felt authorized to avoid the subject pronouns altogether (which are, except in casual speech, made explicit in English) or to avoid conjugation of the verbs, using gerunds instead, in order to create a more haiku-like expression. In *Seaside Pictures*, for example, I chose to avoid the literal translation of 'Miro las estrellas' and to offer instead 'Gazing at the stars.' The parallelistic structure then requires the translator to follow through in subsequent lines 'Gazing at the stars…', 'Gazing at the earth…'.

In the *suites* Lorca went as far as he could in seeking expression in a public form for a personal yearning. He was from the beginning acutely aware of the problem of how to intimate *temblor* (the shiver that comes of suppressed emotion and of contradictory impulses: to move forward or go back, to express desire or keep silent) without turning on the tap of emotion.[64] It seems clear to me that in this early lyric he was never going to be a poet who was content simply to contemplate natural phenomena but that he was going to use his imagination to transform nature and create allegories with it so that his poetry could explore private concerns. As the last *suite* suggests, the possibility for poetic renewal is sought in 'unheard-of landscapes' that are fixed in the narrator's gaze, and the journey to reach those sources of revelation is the journey that will close an important period of self-reflection in Lorca.

On the Spanish editions

Lorca's *suites* still await a critical edition that can account for the many stages and revisions the poems underwent. This anthology is not intended as a step in that direction but, rather, as an introduction and guide to Lorca's project as it unfolded. As Christopher Maurer notes, it may never be possible

---

64   *Temblor* and the related verb *temblar* are recurrent words in the *suites* and crop up in the 1924 song 'Agua, ¿dónde vas?' [Water, where are you bound? (*OC* I, 407–408]. Instead of going upstream or downstream (and all that that symbolizes), the poplar is rooted to one spot and 'trembles' (or 'quakes') with the desire to remain in the moment. The heroine of *Dona Rosita the Spinster* keeps the same *temblor* in the face of her disillusionment (*OC* II, 574).

to settle on a single version of a book of *suite*s; he concludes, with Melissa Dinverno, that several different ones are possible, according to stage and date of composition. This plurality may even be desirable insofar as the versions could reveal how the author responded to different pressures and aims over the years. In establishing an order for this text, I have aimed for a rough chronology based on the careful editorial work of Christopher Maurer and Miguel García-Posada, who were able to improve upon the earlier edition by André Belamich. With one or two exceptions (and these are noted), I have drawn the texts from the *Obras completas* edited by Miguel García-Posada. One or two errors in transmission have been corrected and noted.

RÍO AZUL

BLUE RIVER

[RÍO AZUL]

Río azul.
El barco de marfil
lleva las manzanas
de los besos muertos.
Manzanas de nieve
con el surco tembloroso de los labios.
Río azul.
Y el agua
es una mirada líquida,
un brazo de pupila
infinita.
Río azul.

[BLUE RIVER]

Blue river.
The ivory ship
carries the apples
of extinguished kisses.
Apples of snow
with tremulous lips' furrow.
Blue river.
And the water
is a liquid eye,
a pupil's infinitely
outstretched arm.
Blue river.

SUEÑOS

Todo mi sueño se cierra
como se debe cerrar
un lucero
viejo
que no quiere gastar
su última luz.
Todo mi sueño
pintado por fuera
con mi palabra
vana.

¡Mi sueño!
Granero de estrellas
con sus gusanos
de oro.
¡Mi sueño!
Paseo provinciano
con un banco
desierto.
Doña Distracción
hace girar
sus cien ojos
y una negra figura
se va por el camino
de la lluvia.

Todo mi sueño se cierra.

Las lianas del azul
tocan mi frente.
Ramas nebulosas

DREAMS

All of my dream closes down
the way
an old star
closes
that doesn't care to spend
its last light.
All of my dream
coloured in on the outside
with my useless
words.

My dream!
A granary of stars
with golden
glowworms.
My dream!
A provincial promenade
with a deserted
bench.
Lady Distraction
rolls a hundred eyes
and a black figure
goes down the rainy
highway.

All of my dream closes down.

The tangled vines of blue
brush past my brow.
Nebulous branches

de los abetos
de Jehová,
enturbian el horizonte
casto.

¡Divina confusión
del azul hundido!
Estrellas caídas
sobre la calva de la luna,
penachos de vegetación ideal.
Las otras estrellas
salen del cascarón
y la semilla de un cielo nuevo
se entierra en el infinito
frío.

¡Mi corazón
se llena
de alas!
El ejército
de los recuerdos
se pierde
en el camino
de la Muerte.

En la hoja
de rosa
de la Tierra.
Paso por la ideal selva,
Pulgarcito sin cuento
y sin deseo.

of Jehovah's
old firs
darken
the virgin horizon.

Divine confusion
of the foundering blue!
Fallen stars
on the moon's bald pate,
plumes of ideal vegetation.
The other stars
emerge from their shells
and the seed of a new sky
is buried
in the infinite cold.

My heart
fills
with wings!
An army of memories
scatters
on the road
to Death.

Through the ideal forest, I go,
on the earth's
rose petal.
Little Tom Thumb without a story,
without a desire.

SOLEDAD

Abandono mi vestido
y estrujo mi corazón.
Mi corazón rezuma niebla.
Cuando la selva del azul oculte
la tierra,
mi corazón continuará
empapado de niebla.

SOLITUDE

I shed my garments
and wring out my heart.
It is exuding mist.
When the forest of blue
has hidden the earth,
my heart will still
be drenched in mist.

[RÍO AZUL]

Río azul.
Yo busco mi beso antiguo.
El beso
de mi única hora.
Mi boca, lámpara
apagada,
busca su luz.

Río azul.
Pero había
montones de besos,
moldes de bocas borradas
y besos eternos
adheridos como caracoles
al mástil de marfil.

El barco se detiene.
Hay una tranquilidad sin ritmo
y yo subo a cubierta
con mi traje lírico.

Y los besos extraños,
pompas de jabón
que el alma fabrica,
me ahogan,
mientras el mío huye
por una fría
ceniza boreal.

Río azul.

[BLUE RIVER]

Blue river.
I'm looking for my kiss from long ago.
The kiss
from my only hour.
My mouth, a darkened lamp,
is seeking
its light.

Blue river.
But there were
hundreds of kisses,
moulds of mouths erased
and eternal kisses
stuck like snails
to the ivory mast.

The boat comes to a halt.
A rhythmless lull … and then
I climb on deck
with my lyrical suit.

And those strange kisses,
soap-bubbles
of the heart's manufacture,
are choking me,
while my own kiss flees
through cold
northern ash.

Blue river.

NOCHE

Suite para piano y voz emocionada

NIGHT

A Suite for Piano and for a Voice with Feeling

RASGOS

Aquel camino
sin gente.
Aquel camino.

Aquel grillo
sin hogar.
Aquel grillo.

Y esta esquila
que se duerme.
Esta esquila…

PRELUDIO

El buey
cierra sus ojos
lentamente…
(Calor de establo.)

Este es el preludio
de la noche.

STROKES

That country road
with nobody on it.
That road.

That cricket
without a home.
That cricket.

And this sleepy
cowbell.
This cowbell…

PRELUDE

The ox
slowly
closes his eyes.
(A stable's warmth.)

This is the prelude
to the night.

RINCÓN DEL CIELO

La estrella
vieja
cierra sus ojos turbios.
La estrella
nueva
quiere azular
la sombra.

(En los pinos del monte
hay luciérnagas.)

TOTAL

La mano de la brisa
acaricia la cara del espacio
una vez
y otra vez.
Las estrellas entornan
sus parpados azules
una vez
y otra vez.

A NOOK IN THE SKY

The old
star
shuts her bleary eyes.

The young
star
wants
to wash the shadow blue.

(Fireflies
on the mountain pines.)

THE SUM TOTAL

The breeze
stroking space's brow
again
and again.
The stars' blue eyelids
half-closing,
over and over
again.

UN LUCERO

Hay un lucero quieto,
un lucero sin párpados.
– ¿Dónde?
– Un lucero…
En el agua dormida
del estanque.

FRANJA

El camino de Santiago.
(Oh noche de mi amor,
cuando estaba la pájara pinta
pinta
pinta
en la flor del limón.)

ONE BRIGHT STAR

One star is very still.
It has no eyelids.
– Where?
– A star…
on the sleepy water
of the pond.

SWATH

On the road to Santiago
(Oh night of my love,
when the little red bird
as red as red
can be
perched on the lemon-tree.)

UNA

Aquella estrella romántica
(para las magnolias,
para las rosas).

Aquella estrella romántica
se ha vuelto loca.

Balalín,
balalán.

(Canta, ranita,
en tu choza
de sombra.)

MADRE

La osa mayor
da teta a sus estrellas
panza arriba.
Gruñe
y gruñe.
¡Estrellas niñas, huid;
estrellitas tiernas!

ONE

That romantic little star
(for the magnolias,
for the roses.)
That romantic little star
has lost its wits.

Tralala.
Tralalee.

(Sing, little frog,
in your shadowy
hut.)

MOTHER

The Great Mother Bear is
suckling her stars
belly up.
Growling
and growling.
Little stars, you'd better run away!
Tiny little stars!

RECUERDO

Doña Luna no ha salido.
Está jugando a la rueda
y ella misma se hace burla.
Luna lunera.

HOSPICIO

Y las estrellas pobres,
Las que no tienen luz,

¡qué dolor,
qué dolor,
qué pena!,

están abandonadas
sobre un azul borroso.

¡Qué dolor,
qué dolor,
qué pena!

A MEMORY

Lady Moon has not come out.
She's playing ring around the roses
and she is in the middle.
Moony Moon Lady.

HOSPICE

And the poor little stars,
the ones that have no light.

How terrible,
how terrible.
what a pity!

They've been left all alone
on an uncertain blue.

How terrible,
how terrible,
what a pity!

COMETA

En Sirio
hay niños.

VENUS

Ábrete, sésamo
del día.
Ciérrate, sésamo
de la noche.

ABAJO

El espacio estrellado
se refleja en sonidos.
Lianas espectrales.
Arpa laberíntica.

KITE

There are little kids
on Syrius.

VENUS

Open, sesame
of the day.
Close, sesame
of the night.

BELOW

The starry space
is mirrored in sound.
In spectral vines.
A labyrinth-like harp.

LA GRAN TRISTEZA

No puedes contemplarte
en el mar.
Tus miradas se tronchan
como tallos de luz.
Noche de la tierra.

THE GREAT SADNESS

You cannot look at yourself
in the sea.
Every gaze snaps in two
like stems of light.
Night on earth.

SUITE DE LOS ESPEJOS

MIRROR SUITE

SÍMBOLO

Cristo
tenía un espejo
en cada mano.
Multiplicaba
su propio espectro.
Proyectaba su corazón
en las miradas
negras.
¡Creo!

EL GRAN ESPEJO

Vivimos
bajo el gran espejo.
¡El hombre es azul!
¡Hosanna!

SYMBOL

Christ
held a mirror
in each of his hands.
Multiplying
his own ghost.
Projecting his heart
in the gaze of others,
in their black gazes.
I believe!

THE GREAT LOOKING-GLASS

We live beneath
the great looking-glass.
Mankind is blue!
Hosanna in the highest!

REFLEJO

Doña Luna.
(¿Se ha roto el azogue?)
No.
¿Qué muchacho ha encendido
su linterna?
Sólo una mariposa
basta para apagarte.
Calla…¡pero es posible!
¡Aquella luciérnaga
es la luna!

RAYOS

Todo es abanico.
Hermano, abre los brazos.
Dios es el punto.

REFLECTION

Madam Moon.
(Is the mirror's tain broken?)
No.
What boy has lit
his lantern?
A moth would be enough
to put out your light.
Hush! … How can that be!
That firefly up there
is the moon!

RAYS

Everything is like a fan.
Brother, open your arms.
God is the pivotal point.

RÉPLICA

Un pájaro tan sólo
canta.
El aire multiplica.
Oímos por espejos.

TIERRA

Andamos
sobre un espejo
sin azogue,
sobre un cristal
sin nubes.
Si los lirios nacieran
al revés,
si las rosas nacieran
al revés,
si todas las raíces
miraran las estrellas,
y el muerto no cerrara
sus ojos,
seríamos como cisnes.

REPLICA

But one bird
singing.
In air the multiplications.
We listen through mirrors.

EARTH

We walk
on a silverless
mirror.
On a cloudless
sheet of glass.
If irises grew
backwards,
if roses grew
backwards,
if all the roots
were to gaze at the stars
and the dead man's eyes
did not close,
we would be like swans.

CAPRICHO

Detrás de cada espejo
hay una estrella muerta
y un arco iris niño
que duerme.

Detrás de cada espejo
hay una calma eterna
y un nido de silencios
que no han volado.

El espejo es la momia
del manantial, se cierra,
como concha de luz,
por la noche.

El espejo
es la madre-rocío,
el libro que diseca
los crepúsculos, el eco hecho carne.

CAPRICCIO

Behind every mirror
is a star that has gone out
and a child rainbow,
sleeping.

Behind every mirror,
is an eternal calm
and a nest of silences
that have not taken wing.

A mirror is a mummified
spring, clamping up
at night
like a seashell of light.

A mirror
is the mother of dew,
the book desiccating twilights,
echo made flesh.

SINTO

Campanillas de oro.
Pagoda dragón.
Tilín, tilín,
sobre los arrozales.
Fuente primitiva.
Fuente de la verdad.
A lo lejos,
garzas de color rosa
y el volcán marchito.

SHINTO

Little golden bells.
A dragon pagoda.
Tinkle-tinkle
over the rice paddies.
Primordial fountain,
fountain of truth.
In the distance,
pink herons
and a dried up volcano.

LOS OJOS

En los ojos se abren
infinitos senderos.
Son dos encrucijadas
de la sombra.
La muerte llega siempre
de esos campos ocultos.
(Jardinera que troncha
las flores de las lágrimas.)
Las pupilas no tienen
horizontes.
Nos perdemos en ellas
como en la selva virgen.
Al castillo de irás
y no volverás
se va por el camino
que comienza en el iris.
¡Muchacho sin amor,
Dios te libre de la yedra roja!
¡Guárdate del viajero,
Elenita que bordas
corbatas!

THE EYES

In our eyes infinite paths
open.
Two crossroads
of shadow.
Death always comes
from out of those hidden fields
(a lady gardener lopping off
flowering tears).
Our pupils have
no horizons.
We are lost inside
as if in virgin wood.
This way to the castle
of no return,
on a road beginning in the eyes.
Little loveless boy,
God deliver you from red ivy!
Beware the traveller passing through,
little Helen,
embroidering cravats!

'INITIUM'

Adán y Eva.
La serpiente
partió el espejo
en mil pedazos,
y la manzana
fue la piedra.

'INITIUM'

Adam and Eve.
The snake
smashed the mirror
into a thousand bits,
and the apple
was the rock.

'BERCEUSE' AL ESPEJO DORMIDO

Duerme.
No temas la mirada
errante.
      Duerme.

Ni la mariposa,
ni la palabra,
ni el rayo furtivo
de la cerradura
te herirán.
        Duerme.

Como mi corazón,
así tú,
espejo mío.
Jardín donde el amor
me espera.

Duérmete sin cuidado,
pero despierta,
cuando se muera el último
beso de mis labios.

LULLABY FOR THE SLEEPING MIRROR

Hush now, go to sleep.
Have no fear
of an errant gaze.
                         Sleep.

Neither moth
nor word
nor furtive beam
of keyhole
can hurt you.
                    Sleep.

Like my heart,
so shall you
be, my mirror.
A garden where love
awaits me.

Sleep without a care,
but waken
when the last kiss of my lips
has faded.

AIRE

El aire,
preñado de arcos iris,
rompe sus espejos
sobre la fronda.

CONFUSIÓN

Mi corazón
¿es tu corazón?
¿Quién me refleja pensamientos?
¿Quién me presta
esta pasión
sin raíces?
¿Por qué cambia mi traje
de colores?
¡Todo es encrucijada!
¿Por qué ves en el cielo
tanta estrella?
¿Hermano, eres tú
o soy yo?
¿Y estas manos tan frías
son de aquél?
Me veo por los ocasos,
y un hormiguero de gente
anda por mi corazón.

AIR

The air,
great with rainbows,
shatters its mirrors
over the leaves.

CONFUSION

Is my heart
your heart?
Who bounces thoughts back to me?
Who is it lends me
this passion
without roots?
Why is my many-coloured coat
changing?
Everything is a crossroads!
Why is it you see
so many stars in the sky?
Brother, is that you
or me?
And these hands that are so cold,
do they belong to him?
I see myself in sunsets,
and an anthill of people
troops through my heart.

REMANSO

El búho
deja su meditación,
limpia sus gafas
y suspira.
Una luciérnaga
rueda monte abajo,
y una estrella
se corre.
El búho bate sus alas
y sigue meditando.

POOLING WATER

The owl
stops meditating,
wipes his spectacles,
and sighs.
A firefly
tumbles downhill
and a star
moves aside.
The owl flaps his wings
and resumes his meditation.

EL JARDÍN DE LAS MORENAS

Fragmentos

THE GARDEN OF THE DARK-HAIRED GIRLS

Fragments

PÓRTICO

El agua
toca su tambor
de plata.

Los árboles
tejen el viento
y las rosas lo tiñen
de perfume.

Una araña
inmensa
hace a la luna
estrella.

ACACIA

¿Quién segó el tallo
de la luna?
(Nos dejó raíces
de agua.)
¡Qué fácil nos sería cortar las flores
de la eterna acacia!

PORTICO

The water
taps
its silvery drum.

Trees
weave the wind
and roses leave the stamp
of their perfume.

An enormous spider
makes a star
of the moon.

ACACIA

Who has cut off
the stem of the moon?
(They left us roots
of water.)
How simple it would be to cut the flowers
of the eternal acacia!

ENCUENTRO

María del Reposo,
te vuelvo a encontrar
junto a la fuentefría
del limonar.
¡Viva la rosa en su rosal!

María del Reposo,
te vuelvo a encontrar,
los cabellos de niebla
y ojos de cristal.
¡Viva la rosa en su rosal!

María del Reposo,
Te vuelvo a encontrar.
Aquel guante de luna que olvidé,
¿dónde está?
¡Viva la rosa en su rosal!

ENCOUNTER

María del Reposo,
we meet once again,
beside the cold spring
in the lemon grove.
Long live the rose on its rosebush!

María del Reposo,
we meet once again,
with your locks of mist
and your eyes of glass.
Long live the rose on its rosebush!

María del Reposo,
we meet once again.
That moonlight glove I left behind,
where is it to be found?
Long live the rose on its rosebush!

LIMONAR

Limonar.
Momento
de mi sueño.

Limonar.
Nido
de senos
amarillos.

Limonar.
Senos donde maman
las brisas del mar.

Limonar.
Naranjal desfallecido,
naranjal moribundo,
naranjal sin sangre.

Limonar.
Tú viste mi amor roto
por el hacha de un gesto.

Limonar,
Mi amor niño, mi amor
sin báculo y sin rosa.

Limonar.

LEMON GROVE

Lemon grove.
A moment
in my dream.

Lemon grove.
A nest
of yellow
breasts.

Lemon grove.
Breasts where sea breezes
suckle.

Lemon grove.
Orange grove in a faint,
about to die,
bled out.

Lemon grove.
You saw my love split in two
with the axe of a single gesture.

Lemon grove,
my little boy love,
love without walking-stick or rose.

Lemon grove.

CAPRICHOS

CAPRICCIOS

SOL

¡Sol!
¿Quién te llamó
sol?

A nadie le extrañaría,
digo yo,
ver en el cielo tres letras
en vez de tu cara
de oro.

PIRUETA

Si muriera el alfabeto
morirían todas las cosas.
Las palabras
son las alas.

La vida entera
depende
de cuatro letras.

SUN

Sun!
Who decided to call you
Sun?
Nobody would bat an eye,
I think,
to see three letters in the sky
instead of your gold
face.

PIROUETTE

If the alphabet were to go,
everything else
would go with it: words
are wings.

Life itself
depends
on four letters.

[ÁRBOL]

Árbol.
La *ele* te da las hojas.

Luna.
La *u* te da el color.

Amor.
La *eme* te da los besos.

[TREE]

Tree
The *tee* gives you leaves.

Moon
The *em* gives you colour

Love
The *o* gives you kisses.

MOMENTOS DE CANCIÓN

MOMENTS OF SONG

CANCIÓN CON REFLEJO

En la pradera bailaba
mi corazón.

(Era la sombra
de un ciprés
sobre el viento.)

Y un árbol destrenzaba
la brisa del rocío,
¡la brisa!
Plata del tacto.

Yo decía, ¿recuerdas?

(No me importa
la estrella
ni la rosa.)

¿Recuerdas?

¡Oh palabra perdida!
¡Palabra
sin horizonte!

¿Recuerdas?...

En la pradera bailaba
mi corazón.

(Era la sombra
de un ciprés
en el viento.)

SONG WITH A REFLECTION

In the meadow my heart
danced.

(It was the shadow
of a cypress
on the wind.)

And a tree unplaited
the breeze on the dew.
The breeze!
Silver to the touch.

I said: Do you remember?

(I care for neither
star nor
rose.)

Do you remember…?

Oh a word we've lost!
A word with no
horizon.

Do you remember?

In the meadow my heart
danced.

(It was the shadow
of a cypress
on the wind.)

CANCIÓN SIN ABRIR

Sobre el río
los cínifes.

Sobre el viento
los pájaros.

(Tarde descarriada.)

¡Oh temblor
de mi corazón!

No temas,
me iré lejos
como un eco.

Me iré lejos
en un barco
sin vela
y sin remos.

¡Oh temblor
de mi corazón!

UNOPENED SONG

Over the river,
the mosquitos.

Over the wind,
the birds.

(Straying afternoon.)

Oh the quaking
of my heart!

Don't be afraid,
I'll go far away
like an echo.

I'll go far away,
on a boat
without sails
and oars.

Oh the quaking
of my heart!

SÉSAMO

El reflejo
es lo real.
El río y el cielo
son puertas que nos llevan
a lo Eterno.
Por el cauce de las ranas
o el cauce de los luceros
se irá nuestro amor cantando
la mañana del gran vuelo.
Lo real
es el reflejo.
No hay más que un corazón
y un solo viento.
¡No llorar! Da lo mismo
estar cerca
que lejos.
Naturaleza es
el Narciso eterno.

SESAME

The reflection
is what's real.
River
and sky,
doors that take us
to the Eternal.
On the riverbed of the frogs
or the bright bed of the stars,
when souls are in flight,
our love will be off singing.
What's real
is the reflection.
Nothing here but one heart
and one wind.
Don't cry! It's all the same
to be up close or
far away.
Nature is
the eternal Narcissus.

CANCIÓN BAJO LÁGRIMAS

En aquel sitio,
muchachita de la fuente,
que hay junto al río,
te quitaré la rosa
que te dio mi amigo,
y en aquel sitio,
muchachita de la fuente,
yo te daré mi lirio.
¿Por qué he llorado tanto?
¡Es todo tan sencillo!...
Esto lo haré, ¿no sabes?,
cuando vuelva a ser niño.
¡Ay! ¡ay!
Cuando vuelva a ser niño.

TEARFUL SONG

Over there,
little girl of the fountain,
on that spot beside the river,
I'll take away the rose
my friend gave you,
little girl of the fountain,
and I'll give you my iris.
Why have I cried so hard?
It's all so simple!
This I will do – don't you know? –
when I am a child again.
Oh! Oh!
When I am a child again.

PUESTA DE CANCIÓN

Adolfo en 1921

Después de todo

(la luna
abre su cola
de oro)

…Nada…

(la luna
cierra su cola
de plata.)

Lejos
una estrella
hiere el pavo real
del cielo.

THE SONG SETS

(for Adolfo in 1921)

After all

(the moon
opens
its golden tail)

...It's nothing, never mind…

(the moon
folds
its silver tail up)

Far away
a star
pricks
the peacock heavens.

PAISAJE SIN CANCIÓN

Cielo azul.
Campo amarillo.

Monte azul.
Campo amarillo.

Por la llanura tostada
va caminando un olivo.
Un solo
olivo.

LANDSCAPE WITHOUT SONG

Blue sky.
Yellow country.

Blue hills.
Yellow country.

Through the sunbaked plain
walks a solitary olive-tree.

Just one
olive-tree.

PALIMPSESTOS

A José Moreno Villa

PALIMPSESTS

For José Moreno Villa

I

CIUDAD

El bosque centenario
penetra en la ciudad
pero el bosque está dentro
del mar.

Hay flechas en el aire
y guerreros que van
perdidos entre ramas
de coral.

Sobre las casas nuevas
se mueve un encinar
y tiene el cielo enormes
curvas de cristal.

I

CITY

A centuries-old wood
invades the city
but the forest
is under the sea.

There are arrows in the air
and warriors wandering
amid branches
of coral.

An oak grove hovers
over the new houses
and the sky has
enormous glass curves.

II

CORREDOR

Por los altos corredores
se pasean dos señores

(Cielo
nuevo.
¡Cielo
azul!)

…se pasean dos señores
que antes fueron blancos monjes,

(Cielo
medio.
¡Cielo
morado!*)*

…se pasean dos señores
que antes fueron cazadores.

(Cielo
viejo.
¡Cielo
de oro!)

…se pasean dos señores
que antes fueron…

(Noche.)

II

GALLERY

In the galleries on high
two gentlemen go strolling by

> (A brand-new
> sky.
> Sky of
> blue!)

...Two gentlemen go strolling by
who were once white-robed monks,

> (A middle-aged
> sky.
> Sky of purple
> hue!)

...Two gentlemen go strolling by
who were huntsmen once.

> (Aging
> sky.
> Sky of
> gold!)

…two gentlemen go strolling by
who were once…

> (Night.)

III

PRIMERA PÁGINA

A Isabel Clara, mi ahijada

Fuente clara.
Cielo claro.

¡Oh cómo se agrandan
los pájaros!

Cielo claro.
Fuente clara.

¡Oh cómo relumbran
las naranjas!

Fuente.
Cielo.

¡Oh, cómo el trigo
es tierno!

Cielo.
Fuente.

¡Oh, cómo el trigo
es verde!

III

FIRST PAGE

For Isabel Clara, my god-daughter

Clear spring.
Clear sky.

Oh how the birds
grow in flight!

Clear sky.
Clear spring.

Oh how the oranges
shimmer in the light!

Spring and
sky.

Oh but the wheat
is tender!

Sky
and spring

Oh but the wheat
is green!

CANCIONES BAJO LA LUNA

SONGS BENEATH THE MOON

LUNA LLENA

Al salir

Cuando sale la luna
se pierden las campanas
y aparecen las sendas
de lo impenetrable.

Cuando sale la luna
el mar cubre la tierra,
y el corazón se siente
isla del infinito.

La luna está más lejos
que el sol y las estrellas.
Es perfume y recuerdo,
pompa de azul marchito.

FULL MOON

Rising

When the moon rises
bells go astray
and paths of the impenetrable
appear.

When the moon rises
the sea pours over the earth,
and the heart feels like
an island in the infinite.

The moon is more remote
than the sun and the stars.
It is memory and it is perfume,
a sere blue bubble.

COLORES

Sobre París la luna
tiene color violeta
y se pone amarilla
en las ciudades muertas.

Hay una luna verde
en todas las leyendas,
luna de telaraña
y de rota vidriera.
Y sobre los desiertos
es profunda y sangrienta.

Pero la luna blanca,
la luna verdadera,
sólo luce en los quietos
cementerios de aldea.

CAPRICHO

En la red de la luna,
araña del cielo,
se enredan las estrellas
revoladoras.

COLOURS

The moon over Paris
is a deep violet
and in cities no longer living
it turns yellow.

There's a green moon
in all of the legends,
a cobweb moon and
a moon of broken glass.
And over the deserts
it is deep and bloody.

But the white moon,
the true moon,
you will only find shining
on still village graves.

CAPRICCIO

Fluttering stars
get tangled up
in the net of the moon,
of that spider in the sky.

SALOMÉ Y LA LUNA

La luna es una hermana
de Salomé. (Señora
que en una historia antigua
muerde una muerta boca.)

Salomé era el ocaso.
Un ocaso
de ojos
y de labios.

La luna es el perpetuo
ocaso.
Tarde
continuada
y delirante.

El amor sin orillas
de Salomé al oso
no fue por su palabra;
fue porque su cabeza,
medusa del desierto,
era una luna negra,
una luna imposible,
ahumada y soñolienta.

Salomé es la crisálida
y la luna el capullo,
crisálida de sombra
bajo un palacio oscuro.

SALOMÉ AND THE MOON

The moon is Salomé's
sister. (A lady
in an ancient tale who
bites a dead man's mouth).

Salomé was day
coming to a close, a dying day
of eyes
and lips.

The moon is a perpetual
close of day.
Evening
ongoing and
delirious.

Salomé's boundless love
for the bear
was not because of what he said,
but because his head
was a black moon, like
a medusa in the desert,
an impossible moon,
smoking and somnolent.

Salomé the chrysalis
and the moon the cocoon,
a chrysalis of shadow
under a dark palace.

La luna tiembla sobre el agua,
Salomé tiembla sobre el alma.
¡Oh sublime belleza,
querer hacer de un beso
una estrella!

En el mediodía
o en la noche oscura,
si habláis de Salomé,
saldrá la luna.

The moon shivers on the water,
Salomé shivers on the soul.
Oh, sublime beauty,
to want to turn a kiss
into a star!

At high noon
or the dead of night,
when you speak of Salomé,
the moon begins its climb.

ESTAMPAS DEL MAR

A Emilio y Manolo

SEASIDE PICTURES

For Emilio and Manolo

El mar
quiere levantar
su tapa.

Gigantes de coral
empujan
con sus espaldas.

Y en las cuevas de oro
las sirenas ensayan
una canción que duerma
al agua.

¿Veis las fauces
y las escamas?

Ante el mar
tomad vuestras lanzas.

The sea
wants
to lift its lid.

Giants of coral
shove
with their shoulders.

And in caves of gold
mermaids essay
a song to lull
the waves to sleep.

Can't you see their scales,
their jaws?

When you stand before the sea,
draw your lances!

CONTEMPLACIÓN

Yo evoco
el capitel corintio,
la columna caída
y los pinos.

El mar clásico
canta siempre en Estío
y tiembla como el
capitel corintio.

NOCTURNO

Miro las estrellas
sobre el mar
¡Las estrellas son de agua,
gotas de agua!

Miro las estrellas
sobre mi corazón.
¡Las estrellas son de aroma,
núcleos de aroma!

Miro la tierra
llena de sombra.

CONTEMPLATION

I evoke
the Corinthian capital,
the fallen column
and the pine-trees.

The classical sea
always sings in summer
and furls
like the Corinthian capital.

NOCTURNE

Gazing at the stars
hanging over the sea.
The stars are made of water,
little drops of water!

Gazing at the stars
hanging over my heart.
The stars are orbs of scent,
nuclei of scent!

Gazing at the earth,
brimming with shadow.

GUARDIAS

En el reino del mar
hay dos guardias,
San Cristóbal
y Polifemo.

¡Tres ojos
sobre el viajero errante!

DOS ESTRELLAS DEL MAR

En la torre
de la madrugada
María enseña a Venus
a tejer lana.
Venus le muestra todas
sus miradas
y María se asombra.

En la torre
de la madrugada.

GUARDS

In the kingdom of the sea,
two different men stand guard,
Saint Christopher
and Polyphemus.

Three eyes trained
on the errant traveller!

TWO STARS OF THE SEA

In the tower
of the break of day,
Mary teaches Venus
how to knit wool.
Venus shows her
how to make eyes
and Mary is amazed.

In the tower
of the break of day.

TRES ESTAMPAS DEL CIELO

Dedicadas a la señorita
Argimira López,
que no me quiso

THREE PICTURES OF THE HEAVENS

Dedicated to Miss Argimira López,
who did not love me

I

Las estrellas
no tienen novio.

¡Tan bonitas
como son las estrellas!

Aguardan un galán
que las remonte
a su ideal Venecia.

Todas las noches salen a las rejas
– ¡oh cielo de mil pisos! –
y hacen líricas señas
a los mares de sombra
que las rodean.

Pero aguardar, muchachas,
que cuando yo me muera
os raptaré una a una
en mi jaca de niebla.

I

The stars
don't have sweethearts.

Pretty as
they are!

They're waiting for a suitor
who will take them
to their ideal Venice.
Every night through the bars –
oh thousand-story sky! –
they beckon lyrically
to the shadowy seas
around them.
But just you wait, young ladies,
'cause when I'm gone
I'll carry you off one by one
on a pony made of mist.

II

GALÁN

En todo el cielo
hay un estrello.

Romántico y loco.
Con frac
de polvo
de oro.

¡Pero busca un espejo
para mirar su cuerpo!

¡Oh Narciso de plata
en lo alto del agua!

En todo el cielo
hay un estrello.

II

SUITOR

In the whole of the heavens
there is one boy star.

Romantic and mad.
With a tailcoat
of golden
dust.

He's looking for a mirror
so he can see his body!

Oh Narcissus of silver
high above the water!

In the whole of the heavens
there is one boy star.

III

VENUS

Efectivamente
tienes dos grandes senos
y un collar de perlas
en el cuello.
Un infante de bruma
te sostiene el espejo.

Aunque estás muy lejana,
yo te veo
llevar la mano de iris
a tu sexo,
y arreglar indolente
el almohadón del cielo.

¡Te miramos con lupa,
yo y el Renacimiento!

III

VENUS

In effect
you've two big breasts
and a string of pearls
around your neck.
A hazy prince
holds up your mirror.

Though you are far away
I can see you
place your opaline hand
on your private parts
and lazily plump up
the pillow of the sky.

We are looking at you closely,
the Renaissance and I!

FERIAS

FAIRS

POEMA DE LA FERIA

Bajo el sol de la tuba
pasa la feria
suspirando a los viejos
pegasos cautivos.
La feria
es una rueda.
Una rueda de luces
sobre la noche.

Los círculos concéntricos
del tiovivo llegan,
ondulando la atmósfera
hasta la luna
y hay un niño que pierden
todos los poetas
y una caja de música
sobre la brisa.

POEM OF THE FAIR

Under the sun of the tuba
goes the fair,
sighing after many an
old captive Pegasus.
The fair
is a wheel.
A wheel of lights
turning above the night.

The merry-go-round's
concentric circles
ripple
all the way to the moon
and there is a child
all poets lose track of
and a music box
tinkling in the wind.

CABALLITOS

¡Oh qué pena de caballos
atravesados
por lanzas de caballeros
malos!

Venís a la tierra huyendo
de un cuento al revés, de un campo
lleno de viejos dragones
vencedores de los santos.

De misioneros del sueño
a los campos del diablo
el Señor os envió.
(Dios es un general malo.)

¡Oh qué pena de caballos
atravesados
por lanzas de caballeros
malos!

LITTLE WOODEN HORSES

Oh what a pity the horses
run through
with evil knights'
lances!

You come to earth running
from a story told backwards,
from a field of old dragons
who vanquished the saints.

The Lord has sent you
to the fields of the devil
as missionaries of dream
(A very bad general, God.)

Oh what a pity the horses
run through
with evil knights'
lances!

FERIA ASTRAL

Noche abierta.

Sobre el eje de la luna
gira el tiovivo de Dios.

Sirio el poeta
solloza lejos del tumulto.

Entre las estrellas niñas
baila la Osa Mayor.

Y en las crestas de las frondas
gira el cilindro de la brisa.
En la tienda de la aurora
una estrella viejecita
vende turrón de nieve.

Noche abierta.

THE STARS' FAIR

Night wide-open.

God's carrousel whirls
on the axis of the moon.

The poet Sirius sobs
far from the hew and cry.

Mother Bear dances
amid little girl stars.

And on the leafy canopies
whirls the cylinder of the breeze.
In a booth set up by the dawn
a little old lady star
sells nougat of snow.

Night wide-open.

VERBENA

El que va a la verbena
entra en la casa
de las luciérnagas.

Chin
tata chin
tata chin.

A pesar de que…
no hay más verbena
que la de Cartagena.

Chin
tata chin
tata chin.

¡Qué locura de amor
y de pena!
Y este corazón mío,
¡cómo se deleita,
descubierto,
esperando la flecha!

Chin
tata chin
tata chin.

STREET FAIR

Whoever goes to the fair
visits the house
of fireflies.

   Clank
   Clankety
   Clank

Even if…
the only real *verbena*
is the one in Cartagena.

   Clank
   Clankety
   Clank

What madness of love,
what a shame!
This heart of mine,
revelling in pain,
flung open
to the arrow!

   Clank
   Clankety
   Clank

GRITO

Cínife,
mariposa,
pájaro,
estrella.

¿Qué?

Estrella,
pájaro,
mariposa,
cínife.

Ya en el suelo
mi corazón atravesado
vuela sobre las muchachas
de la feria.

CRY

Mosquito,
moth,
bird,
star.

What?

Star,
bird,
moth,
mosquito.

On the ground now
my heart is run through
and sails over the girls
at the fair.

TAMBOR

El tambor
es el corazón
de la feria.
Un corazón marchito
que late como si fuera
de un niño.

Ningún músico
lo ha visto.
Él es el verdadero
Pierrot, que canta lírico
a la luna, que cabe
dentro de un anillo
con una melodía
de amor desconocido.

El tambor tiene una luz
de pergamino
(musical fuego fatuo)
y en las noches de estío
mil mariposas viejas
persiguen sus latidos.

DRUM

The drum
is the heart
of the fair.
A leathery heart
that beats as if
it were a child's.

No musician has seen this.
He is the true Pierrot,
who sings so lyrically
to the moon, who fits
inside its ring
with a melody
of unheard-of love.

The drum has a
parchment gleam
(musical will-o-the-wisp)
and on summer nights
a thousand old moths
home in on its heartbeat.

El tambor es la nostalgia
del camino.
Suena a cielo con nubes
y a lejanía infinita.
En el barco encallado
del circo
o en el aire campesino
¡late!
¡Oh ataúd de la luna
llena!

The drum is nostalgia
for the open road.
It sounds like
the sky with clouds,
infinitely removed from us.
In the circus (a boat
run aground)
or in the country air,
it beats!
Oh casket
of the full moon!

ROSAS DE PAPEL

Aquel hombre
de la constelación inmensa,
Atlante,
de multicolor estrella,
va perdido entre las llagas
de las antorchas.
Aquel hombre
de la nube de risas
lleva
rosas para los vientos
de la infancia.
Y aquel hombre,
fantasma del otoño,
se reserva
las rosas de los niños
muertos
y se las manda
en una cometa.

PAPER ROSES

That man
from an immense constellation,
an Atlas
of a many-coloured star,
is lost amid the torches'
open wounds.
That man, the one that hails
from a cloud of laughter
is bearing roses
for the winds
of childhood.
And that same man,
a phantom of autumn,
is saving roses
for all the dead children,
to send to them on a kite.

LUNA DE FERIA

La luna
no se ve en las ferias.
¡Hay demasiadas lunas
sobre el césped!

Todo juega a ser luna.
La misma feria
es una luna herida
que cayó en la ciudad.

Lunas microscópicas
bailan en los cristales
y algunas se detienen
sobre los nubarrones
de la charanga.

La luna del azul
no se ve en las ferias.
Se vela suspirando:
'¡Me duelen los ojos!'

FAIRGROUND MOON

You cannot see
the moon at the fair.
There are too many moons
performing on the lawn!

Everything pretends
it is the moon. The fair itself
is a wounded moon
fallen on top of the city.

Microscopic moons
dance on the windows
and some of them linger
on the brass band's clouds.

The blue-sky moon
is nowhere to be seen.
It lowers its veil and sighs:
'How this hurts my eyes!'

CANCIÓN MORENA

Me perdería
por tu país moreno,
María del Carmen.

Me perdería
por tus ojos sin nadie,
pulsando los teclados
de tu boca inefable.

En tu abrazo perpetuo
sería moreno el aire
y tendría la brisa
el vello de tu carne.

Me perdería
en tu país moreno,
María del Carmen.

DARK-HAIRED SONG

I could lose my way
in your dark country,
María del Carmen.

I could lose my way
in those eyes reflecting nobody,
as I play the keys
of your ineffable mouth.

The air would be dark
in your perpetual embrace
and the wind would feel like
the down on your flesh.

I could lose my way
in your dark country,
María del Carmen.

COLUMPIO

La niña va en el columpio
de norte a sur
de sur a norte.

En la parábola
tiembla una estrella roja
bajo todas las estrellas.

CONFUSIÓN

Sobre las casas despiertas
van serpentinas sonoras.

¡Rojas – amarillas – verdes!

La placeta está inundada
por los caños de los pitos.

¡Rojos – amarillos – verdes!

Las gentes van descarriadas
por laberintos de música.

¡Azules – rosas – azules!

Y el reloj no tiene hora
ni las pupilas miradas.

¡Negras – negras – negras!

SWING

On the swing
north to south,
south to north
goes the little girl.

A red star shivers
below all the others,
on the parabola.

CONFUSION

Noisy streamers sail
over unsleeping houses.

Red–yellow–green!

The little square is inundated
with whistles.

Red–yellow–green!

People move distractedly
through labyrinthine tunes.

Blue–pink–blue!

And the clock does not tell time
nor do the eyes see.

Black–black–black!

OCASO DE FERIA

Los balcones se cierran
para enjaular los besos.

¡Oh cuánta estrella,
cuánta estrella!

Se va apagando en el aire
un aristón moribundo.

¡Más estrellas,
más estrellas!

Pero los pobres pegasos
no pueden cerrar sus ojos.

¡Oh la única
estrella!

THE FAIR GOES DOWN

The balconies are shuttered
to keep kisses in a cage.

> Oh how many stars there are!
> How many!

A dying hurdy-gurdy
slowly fades in the wind.

> More stars!
> Even more!

But the poor little Pegasus ponies
cannot close their eyes.

> Oh, the only
> star in the sky!

VARIACIÓN

Trino (final)

Ante la feria desierta
el poeta suspira.
(El viento bate las lonas.)

Y por las frondas verdes
un pájaro se va.
Pájaro de Mambrún,
pájaro sin hogar,
cantando el pío pío,
cantando el pío pa.

VARIATION

(Final trill)

The poet sighs
before the deserted fairground.

(Tents flap in the wind.)

And through the leafy canopy
a bird takes wing.
The bird that was Mambrú's,
a bird that has no home,
singing tweet tweet tweet
tweet tweet tweet a-roo!

SOMBRA

SHADOW

PUEBLO

Entre tejado y tejado
va el alto río del cielo.

Sobre las acacias viejas
duermen pájaros errantes.

Y la torre sin campanas
(Santa Lucía de piedra)
se afirma en la tierra dura.

VILLAGE

From rooftop to rooftop
flows the sky's high river.

On the old acacias
errant birds doze.

And the tower without bells
(Saint Lucy of stone)
stands firm on the hard earth.

MEMENTO

Cuando muramos
nos llevaremos
una serie de vistas
del cielo.

(Cielos de amanecer
y cielos nocturnos.)

Aunque me han dicho
que muertos
no se tiene
más recuerdo
que el de un cielo de Estío,
un cielo negro
estremecido
por el viento.

MURCIÉLAGO

El murciélago,
elixir de la sombra.
verdadero amante de la estrella,
muerde el talón del día.

MEMENTO

When we die
we will take with us
a series of
views of the sky.

(Skies at daybreak
and skies at night.)

Though they tell me that
when you are dead
all you remember
is
the sky in summer,
a black sky
rattled
by the wind.

BAT

The bat,
an elixir of shadow,
the star's true lover,
nips at the heel of day.

FIN

Ya pasó
el fin del mundo
y ha sido
el juicio tremendo.
Ya ocurrió catástrofe
de los luceros.

El cielo de la noche
es un desierto,
un desierto de lámparas
sin dueño.

Muchedumbres de plata
se fueron
a la densa levadura
del misterio.

Y en el barco de la Muerte
vamos los hombres, sintiendo
que jugamos a la vida,
¡que somos espectros!

Mirando a los cuatro puntos
todo está muerto.
El cielo de la noche
es una ruina,
un eco.

ENDING

The end of the world
is over now
and the momentous judgement
is past.
The disaster of the stars
has come and gone.

And the night sky
is a desert,
a desert of lamps
without owner.

Silvery crowds
have departed
for the dense leaven
of mystery.

And on Death's ferry
go we humans,
feeling we play at life, that
we are spectres!

Gazing at the four compass points;
everything is dead.
The night sky is
a ruin,
an echo.

OSA MAYOR

Juguete
    Éramos siete.
    ¿Dónde estamos?

Da tristeza
ver el carro
sin auriga
ni caballos.

Sobre el cielo
da una pena
suave verte soñando
con un camino de oro
y boreales caballos.

Sobre el negro cristalino
¡qué harás cuando tengas, carro,
con la lluvia de los tiempos
tus luceros oxidados!
¿No piensas nunca meterte
bajo techado?
Yo te unciría una noche
a dos grandes bueyes blancos.

URSA MAJOR

Plaything
  There were seven of us.
  Where are we?

It is sad
to see the chariot
without driver
or horses.

Over the sky
it is a little sad
to see you dreaming
of a golden road
and horses of northern lights.

Over the crystalline black
what will you do, chariot,
when your stars are rusted
in the rain of time?
Don't you ever think
of going inside?
One of these nights I would yoke you
to two big white oxen.

PONIENTE

Sobre el cielo exquisito,
más allá del violado,
hay nubes desgarradas
como camelias grises,
y un deseo de alas
sobre las crestas frías.

Un ocaso teñido
de sobra como este
dará una noche inmensa
sin brisa ni caminos.

WEST

Across the exquisite sky,
far beyond the violet,
there are tattered clouds
like grey camellias
and on cold mountain peaks
a yearning for wings.

A sunset tinged
with shadow like this
will forge an immense night
without wind or roads.

CUMBRE

Cuando llegue a la cumbre…

(Oh corazón desolado,
San Sebastián de Cupido.)

Cuando llegue a la cumbre…

¡Dejadme cantar!

Porque cantando
no veré los oteros sombríos
ni los rebaños
que en lo profundo van
sin pastores.
Cantando,
veré la única estrella
que no existe.

Cuando llegue a la cumbre…
cantando.

SUMMIT

When I get to the mountaintop…

(Oh desolate heart,
Cupid Saint Sebastian.)

When I get to the mountaintop…

Let me sing!

Because singing
I will not see the darkened hills
or down below
flocks without their shepherds.
Singing I will see
the only star
that doesn't exist.

When I get to the mountaintop…
singing.

SAUCE

¡Jeremías
exquisito!

Las lágrimas asoman
por tus ojos fríos,
mas tu llanto no rueda
sobre el camino.

Abres bajo tus ramas
un abismo
y matizas con gestos
el color vespertino.

¡Oh Jeremías
exquisito!

WILLOW

Exquisite
Jeremiah!

Tears come
to your cold eyes
but your sobbing does not spill
along the road.

Under your boughs you open
an abyss
and your gestures give a different tone
to the colour of evening.

Oh exquisite
Jeremiah!

CUATRO BALADAS AMARILLAS

A Claudio Guillén

FOUR YELLOW BALLADS

For Claudio Guillén

I

En lo alto de aquel monte
hay un arbolito verde.

Pastor que vas,
pastor que vienes.

Olivares soñolientos
bajan al llano caliente.

Pastor que vas,
pastor que vienes.

Ni ovejas blancas ni perro
ni cayado ni amor tienes.

Pastor que vas.

Como una sombra de oro
en el trigal te disuelves.

Pastor que vienes.

I

High on that hill
is a little green tree.

Shepherd who comes,
shepherd who goes.

Sleepy olive groves
step down the sun-warmed plain.

Shepherd who comes,
shepherd who goes.

Neither dog nor white sheep,
nor crook nor love have you.

Shepherd who goes.

Like a shadow of gold
you melt into the wheat.

Shepherd who comes.

II

La tierra estaba
amarilla.

   Orillo, orillo,
   pastorcillo.

Ni luna blanca
ni estrellas lucían.

   Orillo, orillo,
   pastorcillo.

Vendimiadora morena
corta el llanto de la viña.

   Orillo, orillo,
   pastorcillo.

II

The earth was
yellow.

A golden selvage,
shepherd boy.

Neither moon nor star
shone in the sky.

A golden selvage,
shepherd boy.

A dark-haired harvester
cuts teardrops from the vine.

A golden selvage,
shepherd boy.

III

Dos bueyes rojos
en el campo de oro.

Los bueyes tienen ritmo
de campanas antiguas
y ojos de pájaro.
Son para las mañanas
de niebla, y sin embargo
horadan la naranja
del aire, en el verano.
Viejos desde que nacen
no tienen amo
y recuerdan las alas
de sus costados.
Los bueyes
siempre van suspirando
por los campos de Ruth
en busca del vado,
borrachos de luceros
a rumiarse sus llantos.

Dos bueyes rojos
en el campo de oro.

III

Two red oxen
on a field of gold.

The oxen have the rhythm
of old bells
and birds' eyes.
They're for mornings
of mist; and yet
they pierce the orange
of the summer air.
Old since birth,
they have no master.
And they remember the wings
they had on their sides.
Oxen always
go sighingly
through the fields of Ruth,
in search of a ford,
the eternal ford,
drunk with stars,
ruminating tears.

Two red oxen
on a field of gold.

IV

Sobre el cielo
de las margaritas ando.

Yo imagino esta tarde
que soy santo.
Me pusieron la luna
en las manos.
Yo la puse otra vez
en los espacios
y el Señor me premió
con la rosa y el halo.

Sobre el cielo
de las margaritas ando.

Y ahora voy
por este campo
a librar a las niñas
de galanes malos
y dar monedas de oro
a todos los muchachos.

Sobre el cielo
de las margaritas ando.

IV

Over the daisy-eyed heavens
go I.

I imagine this evening
they've made me a saint.
They put the moon
in my hands.
I put it back
in its place
and the Lord offered recompense
with a halo and a rose.

Over the daisy-eyed heavens
go I.

And now
I go through this field
to deliver young girls
from dishonourable swains
and hand out gold coins
to all the young men.

Over the daisy-eyed heavens
go I.

REMANSOS

POOLS IN THE STREAM

REMANSOS

Ciprés.
(Agua estancada.)

Chopo.
(Agua cristalina.)

Mimbre.
(Agua profunda.)

Corazón.
(Agua de pupila.)

REMANSILLO

Me miré en tus ojos
pensando en tu alma.

Adelfa blanca.

Me miré en tus ojos
Pensando en tu boca.

Adelfa roja.

Me miré en tus ojos.
¡Pero estabas muerta!

Adelfa negra.

POOLS IN THE STREAM

Cypress-tree.
(Still water.)

Aspen.
(Crystal-clear.)

Wicker.
(Deep water.)

Heart.
(Water of the eye.)

LITTLE POOL

I gazed into your eyes
thinking of your soul.

White oleander.

I gazed into your eyes
thinking of your mouth.

Red oleander.

I gazed into your eyes.
But you were not alive!

Black oleander.

VARIACIÓN

El remanso del aire
bajo la rama del eco.

El remanso del agua
bajo fronda de luceros.

El remanso de tu boca
bajo espesura de besos.

VARIATION

The still air
beneath the bough of an echo.

The still water
beneath a frond of stars.

Your still mouth
beneath a thicket of kisses.

REMANSO, CANCIÓN FINAL

Ya viene la noche.

Golpean rayos de luna
sobre el yunque de la tarde.

Ya viene la noche.

Un árbol grande se abriga
con palabras de cantares.

Ya viene la noche.

Si tu vinieras a verme
por los senderos del aire.

Ya viene la noche.

Me encontrarías llorando
bajo los álamos grandes.
¡Ay morena!
Bajo los álamos grandes.

MEDIA LUNA

La luna va por el agua.
¿Cómo está el cielo tranquilo?
Va segando lentamente
el temblor viejo del río
mientras que una rana joven
la toma por espejito.

POOL, FINAL SONG

Here comes the night.

Moonbeams beat
on the anvil of the evening.

Here comes the night.

An old tree bundles up
in the words of ancient song.

Here comes the night.

If you were to come see me
over the paths of the air.

Here comes the night.

You would find me weeping
under the great poplars.
Oh dark-haired girl!
Under the great poplars.

HALF-MOON

The moon proceeds along the water.
How is it the sky is serene?
Slowly she mows away
the river's old tremors
while a young frog
takes her for a mirror.

HORAS DE VERANO

SUMMER HOURS

[AFILADOR]

Afilador.
(Las tres.)
El alma de Pan
en los labios
del afilador.

¡Qué tristeza
tan polvorienta!

Evoca
un verde remanso
y una cadera
entre las ramas.

El hombre lleva
la rueda
de Santa Catalina.

¡Qué tristeza!

[KNIFEGRINDER]

Knifegrinder.
(Three o'clock.)
Pan's soul
is on the lips
of the knifegrinder.

Such a dusty
sadness!

The sound evokes
a sleepy green pool
and a hip
among the branches.

The man is carrying
a catherine
wheel.

Such sadness!

LAS CINCO

Potro

Por la calle sin gente
pasa un caballo negro,
el caballo errabundo
de los malos sueños.

El aire del poniente
viene a lo lejos,
una ventana gime
con el viento.

LAS SEIS

Los pájaros empujan
a la tarde
y llevan con sus picos
la cola azul del día.

El ocaso tatuado
de veletas
sostiene la barca
de la media luna.

Y en la fuente fría
canta la culebra.

FIVE O'CLOCK

Colt

Through the empty street
rides a black horse,
the errant horse
of troubled dreams.

A breeze from the west
off in the distance;
in the wind
a window moans.

SIX O'CLOCK

Birds nudge
the afternoon along,
the day's blue tail.
in their beaks.

A sunset tattooed
with weather-vanes
buoys up the boat
of the half-moon.

And in the coldwater spring
a snake is singing.

LAS SIETE

La primera estrella.
Todo mira hacia Venus
y ella como una niña
que se cae en el aljibe
tiembla y tiembla
como diciendo:
¿Volveré mañana?

LAS OCHO

El cielo se arrancó
la venda
y el dragón de los mil ojos
nos lame con sus lenguas
de viento.

Venus se extravía
por las muchedumbres
y yo me acuerdo de una novia
que no he tenido nunca.

SEVEN O'CLOCK

The first star is out.
Everything looks Venus's way,
and like a little girl
who has fallen into the cistern,
she trembles and trembles
as if to say,
Will I be back again tomorrow?

EIGHT O'CLOCK

The sky tore
its blindfold off
and the thousand-eyed dragon
licks at us
in gusts of wind.

Venus is lost
in the crowd and I
recall a sweetheart
I never had.

LAS NUEVE

Azul sin sangre.
Aire de terciopelo.

¡Oh amiga mía!
Podemos
bajar a la cisterna del corazón,
podemos
por el río de las palabras
llegar a la isla
del beso.
Podemos
hundirnos en el olivar
sediento.

VILANO DE NOCHE

Sobre el agua
que late entre las zarzas
las estrellas
se alargan.

NINE O'CLOCK

Blue without a drop of blood.
The air like velvet.

Oh my love!
We can dip down
to the heart's
cistern. We can take
the river of words
to the island of a kiss.

We can
plunge into
the thirsty olive grove.

THISTLE DOWN, NIGHT

On the water
that quickens among the brambles
the stars
grow longer.

EL REGRESO

THE RETURN

EL REGRESO

Yo vuelvo
por mis alas.

¡Dejadme volver!

¡Quiero morirme siendo
amanecer!

¡Quiero morirme siendo
ayer!

Yo vuelvo
por mis alas.

¡Dejadme retornar!

Quiero morirme siendo
manantial.

Quiero morirme fuera
de la mar.

THE RETURN

> I'm going back
> for my wings.

Let me go back!

I want to die while I am
dawn!

I want to die when
yesterday!

> I'm going back
> for my wings.

Let me go back!

I want to die
at the source of the stream.

I want to die
away from the sea.

CORRIENTE

El que camina
se enturbia.

El agua corriente
no ve las estrellas.

El que camina
se olvida.

Y el que se para
sueña.

CURRENT

He who moves along
grows muddy.

Running water
doesn't see the stars.

He who moves along
forgets who he is.

And he who pauses
dreams.

HACIA...

Vuelve,
¡corazón!,
vuelve.

Por las selvas del amor
no verás gentes.
Tendrás claros manantiales.
En lo verde
hallarás la rosa inmensa
del siempre.

Y dirás: ¡Amor!, ¡amor!,
sin que tu herida
se cierre.

Vuelve,
¡corazón mío!,
vuelve.

TOWARDS...

    Go back,
    heart!
    Go back.

In the forest of love
you won't see people,
you'll have clear-flowing springs.
In the green
you will find
the immense rose of forever.

And you will say: Love! Love!
without your wound
ever closing up.

    Go back,
    heart!
    Go back.

RECODO

Quiero volver a la infancia
y de la infancia a la sombra.

¿Te vas, ruiseñor?
Vete.

Quiero volver a la sombra
y de la sombra a la flor.

¿Te vas, aroma?
¡Vete!

Quiero volver a la flor
y de la flor
a mi corazón.

¿Te vas, amor?
¡Adiós!

(¡A mi desierto corazón!)

BEND IN THE RIVER

I want to go back to childhood
and from childhood to shadow.

　Are you leaving, nightingale?
　Then go.

I want to go back to shadow
and from shadow to flower.

　Are you leaving, fragrance?
　Then go.

I want to go back to the flower
and from the flower
to my heart.

　Are you leaving, love?
　Goodbye!

(To my desert heart!)

DESPEDIDA

Me despediré
en la encrucijada
para entrar en el camino
de mi alma.

Despertando recuerdos
y horas malas
llegaré al huertecillo
de mi canción blanca
y me echaré a temblar como
la estrella de la mañana.

FAREWELL

I'll say goodbye
at the crossroads
in order to go down
the path of my soul.

Stirring up memories
and troubled moments
I'll make my way to the little garden
of my white song
and I'll go all atremble
like the morning star.

RÁFAGA

Pasaba mi niña,
¡qué bonita iba!,
con su vestidito
de muselina
y una mariposa
prendida.

¡Síguela, muchacho,
la vereda arriba!
Y si ves que llora
o medita,
píntale el corazón
con purpurina
y dile que no llore
si queda solita.

GUST OF WIND

My little girl was going by.
How pretty she looked!
With her little
muslin frock.
And a butterfly pinned
on top.

Follow her, boy,
way up the path!
If you see she is tearful
or starting to brood
paint her heart
a glittering gold
and tell her not to cry
if she's left all alone.

SECRETOS

SECRETS

FUENTE

Ante la fuente fría
Cristo medita
con una semilla
entre las manos.

(Está sediento el cauce
de la brisa.)

Ante la fuente clara
Cristo y su alma
luchan por la palabra
que duerme todavía.
¡Pero la fuente mana!

PAN

¡Ved qué locura!
Los cuernos de Pan
se han vuelto alas
y como una mariposa
enorme
vuela por su selva
de fuego.
¡Ved qué locura!

FOUNTAIN

At the coldwater spring
Christ is brooding,
cupping a seed
in his hands.

(The breeze's bed
is thirsty.)

At the clearwater spring
Christ and his soul
struggle to articulate
a still dormant word.
Yet the springwater flows!

PAN

Look what madness!
Pan's two horns
have turned into wings
and like a gigantic
butterfly he flits
through his fiery
forest.
Look what madness!

LEÑADOR

En el crepúsculo
yo caminaba.
¿'Dónde vas?', me decían.
'A cazar estrellas claras.'
Y cuando las colinas
dormían, regresaba
con todas las estrellas
en la espalda.
¡Todo el haz
de la noche blanca!

ESPEJO

Mi cintillo de oro
se perdió en el espejo.
(Quiero decir
que nunca existió.)

En los espejos se pierden
Las cosas que no existen.

Mi cintillo era de oro:
¿de sol o de margaritas?

¿Qué mujer me lo dio?
Preguntárselo a mi espejo.

Por … más … que…
¡yo no tengo espejo!

WOODCUTTER

I walked on
through the dusk.
'Where are you going?', they asked.
'To hunt the shining stars.'
And when the hills slept,
I came back
with all of the stars
slung over my shoulder.
The whole bundle belonging
to the white night!

MIRROR

My little golden sash
got lost in the looking-glass.
(I mean, it never
existed.)

(In mirrors things get lost
that never really were.)

My little sash:
of golden sun or daisies?

What lady gave it me?
Go and ask the looking-glass.

Even … if ... I don't really
have a glass at all!

PUERTA ABIERTA

Las puertas abiertas
dan siempre a una sima
mucho más profunda
si la casa es vieja.

La puerta
no es puerta
hasta que un muerto
sale por ella
y mira doliente, crucificada,
a la madrugada sanguinolenta.

¡Qué trabajo nos cuesta
traspasar los umbrales
de todas las puertas!
Vemos dentro una lámpara
ciega
o una niña que teme
las tormentas.

La puerta es siempre la clave
de la leyenda.
Rosa de dos pétalos
que el viento abre
y cierra.

OPEN DOOR

Open doors
always give onto a chasm
all the deeper
if the house is old.

A door
is not a door
until a dead man
goes through, gazing
in sorrow at the blood
of the crucified morning.

How hard for us
to cross the thresholds
of all doorways!
Inside we see a
blacked-out lamp
or a girl who is afraid
of storms.

The door is always the key
to the legend.
Rose of two petals
opening and closing
in the wind.

VIAJE

He visto las colas del viento,
las flores de la brisa.
He visto el pájaro Grifón
y la torre de Delgadina.

¿De dónde vienes,
de dónde?

He visto un camino azul
y unas niñas
que iban cantando el romance
de la verde oliva.

¿No sabes de dónde vengo,
niña mía?
Pues…de tu última
sonrisa.

JOURNEY

I have seen the wind's coat-tails,
the breeze's flowers.
I've seen the Griffin bird
and Delgadina's tower.

Where do you come from,
where?

I have seen a blue road
and little girls singing
the ballad of the green olive tree.

Don't you know where I come from,
little girl?
I come from the country
of your last smile.

BOTICA

¿Esos venenos
son de la India?

¿Y esos perfumes
son de la Arabia?

(El boticario solloza
junto a su niño muerto.)

¿Aquel bálsamo cura
heridas de amor?

¿Y el agua sonrosada
de la juventud?

(El boticario se inclina
sobre su niño muerto.)

Dígame: ¿Alguna rosa
da un veneno violento?

¿Qué tiene esa redoma?
¿No ve usted cómo tiembla?

……………………….

(Entre los sollozos
se oye un batir de alas
dentro de todos los frascos.)

APOTHECARY

Are those poisons
from India?

And are those perfumes
Arabian?

(The chemist is sobbing
at his dead child's side.)

Does that balsam heal
the wounds of love?

And is that the rosy
water of youth?

(The chemist stoops
over his dead child.)

Tell me: do some roses
give off a poisonous fume?

What is in that jar?
Can't you see how it shakes?

………………………………

(Amid the sobbing
can be heard the beating of wings
inside all the bottles.)

DONCELLITA

¿Por qué te recuerdo
bajo una lluvia de Marzo
al salir del colegio?

Pajarita de las nieves
te llamaban. Un interno
te dio su rosa. Luego
se te cayó la pluma
con que escribo los versos.
Tan pequeñita, y tú
¡sin saberlo!

LITTLE MAID

Why do I remember you
one rainy day in March
coming out of school?

Little snowbird,
they called you. One boarder
gave you his rose. Then
you lost the quill
I use to write these lines.
So little and you
none the wiser!

ÁLBUM BLANCO

A Claudio de la Torre

Eloísa López tenía un álbum sin escribir. Y se ha muerto. ¡Pobrecita! Pero yo se lo escribo con tinta blanca. Ruego a los lectores una oración por su alma. El arzobispo de Constantinopla se ha dignado conceder 100 días de indulgencia. ¡Ah! Si ustedes la hubiesen conocido…

WHITE ALBUM

Eloísa López had an album that no one had written in. And she is dead. Poor little thing! But I am going to write something in white ink in her album. I beg readers to say a prayer for her soul. The Archbishop of Constantinople has seen fit to offer 100 days' indulgence. Ah! If you had only known her…

PRIMERA PÁGINA

Cerezo en flor

En Marzo
te marchas a la luna.
Dejas aquí tu sombra.
Las praderas se tornan
irreales.
Llueven pájaros blancos.
Y yo me pierdo en tu bosque
gritando:
¡Ábrete, sésamo!
¡Seré niño?
Gritando:
¡Ábrete, sésamo!

FIRST PAGE

Cherry tree in bloom

In March
you are off to the moon.
Leaving behind your shadow.
The meadows become
unreal,
raining white birds,
and I am lost
in your woods, shouting,
'Open, sesame!
Am I a child still?
Shouting:
'Open, sesame!'

SEGUNDA PÁGINA

Cisne

Ni Pan
ni Leda.

(Sobre tus alas
se duerme la luna llena.)

Ni bosque
ni siringa.

(Por tu plumaje
resbala la noche fría.)

Ni carne rubia
ni besos.

(De escarcha y sueño remolcas
a la barca de los muertos.)

SECOND PAGE

Swan

Neither Pan
nor Leda.

(The full moon sleeps
on your wings.)

Neither wood
nor pan-pipe.

(The cold night slides
over your feathers.)

Neither golden flesh
nor kisses.

(Of frost and dream, you
tow the boat of the dead.)

TERCERA PÁGINA

Inventos

(Estrellas de la nieve)

Hay montañas
que quieren ser
de agua,
y se inventan estrellas
sobre la espalda.

(Nubes)

Y hay montañas
que quieren tener
alas
y se inventan las nubes
blancas.

THIRD PAGE

Inventions

(*Snow stars*)

There are mountains
that long to be
made of water,
and they invent stars
to wear on their backs.

(Clouds)

And there are mountains
that long to have
wings,
and they invent
the white clouds.

CUARTA PÁGINA

Nieve

Las estrellas
se están desnudando.
Camisas de estrellas
caen sobre el campo.

QUINTA PÁGINA

Amanece

La cresta del día
asoma.
Cresta blanca
de un gallo de oro.

La cresta de mi risa
asoma.
Cresta de oro
de un gallo de sombra.

FOURTH PAGE

Snow

The stars
are disrobing.
Star chemises
fall onto the fields.

FIFTH PAGE

Daybreak

The crest of the day
peeps out.
The white crest
of a golden cock.

The crest of my laughter
peeps out.
The golden crest
of a shadowy cock.

ÚLTIMA PÁGINA

Baladilla de Eloisa muerta
(Palabras de un estudiante)

Estabas muerta,
como al final
de todas las novelas.
Yo no te amaba, Eloisa.
¡Y eras tan tierna!
Con música de Bécquer
o de Espronceda,
tú me soñabas guapo
con melena,
y yo te daba besos
sin darme cuenta
de que no te decía:
¡oh labios de cereza!
Qué gran romántica
eras.
Bebías vinagre a escondidas
de tu abuela.
Te pusiste como una
celinda de primavera.
Y yo estaba enamorado
de otra. ¿No ves qué pena?
De otra que estaba escribiendo
un nombre sobre la arena.

LAST PAGE

Little Ballad of the Dead Eloisa
(A Student's Words)

You were dead,
just like at the end
of all the novels.
I did not love you, Eloisa.
And you were so sweet!
You pictured me handsome
and long-haired,
with background music by
Bécquer or Espronceda
and I kissed you
without realizing
I had not said:
Oh your cherry lips!
What a great romantic
heroine you were.
Drinking vinegar
behind Grandmother's back.
You were thin
as a reed in the spring.
And I was in love
with another.
Can't you see what a shame?
Someone who was writing
a name in the sand.

Cuando yo llegué a tu casa
estabas muerta
entre cirios y entre albahacas,
igual que en las novelas.
Rodeaban tu barquita
las niñas de tu escuela.
Habías bebido el vinagre
de la botella eterna.

Tilín talán
Te lloraban
las campanas tiernas.

Talán, tilín
en la tarde
con dolor de cabeza.
Quizá soñabas durmiendo
que eras Ofelia
sobre un lago azul de agua
calenturienta.

Tilín, talán
¡que te lloren
las campanas tiernas!

¡Talán, tilín
en la tarde
con dolor de cabeza!

When I got to your home
you were dead
amid candles and sweet basil,
just like in the novels.
The girls from school
gathered round your little boat.
You had drunk the vinegar
of the everlasting.

Tinkle tinkle
The little bells
mourned you.

Tinkle tinkle
in the afternoon
with an aching head.
Perhaps you lay dreaming
you were Ophelia
on a blue lake of
feverish water.

Tinkle tinkle
May the little bells
mourn you!

Tinkle tinkle
in the afternoon
with an aching head!

LA SELVA DE LOS RELOJES

THE FOREST OF CLOCKS

LA SELVA DE LOS RELOJES

Entré en la selva
de los relojes.

Frondas de tic-tac,
racimos de campanas
y bajo la hora múltiple,
constelaciones de péndulos.

Los lirios negros
de las horas muertas,
los lirios negros
de las horas niñas.
¡Todo igual!
¿Y el oro del amor?

Hay una hora tan sólo.
¡Una hora tan sólo!
¡La hora fría!

THE FOREST OF CLOCKS

I went into the forest
of clocks.

Fronds going tick-tock,
bunches of bells,
and under a multiplying hour,
constellations of pendulums.

The black irises
of vacant hours,

The black irises
of nursery time.
All one and the same!
And the gold of love?

There is but one hour!
One hour!
The cold hour!

MALEZA

Me interné
por la hora mortal.
Hora de agonizante
y de últimos besos.
Grave hora en que sueñan
las campanas cautivas.

Relojes de cuco,
sin cuco.
Estrella mohosa
y enormes mariposas
pálidas.

Entre el boscaje
de suspiros
el aristón
sonaba
que tenía cuando niño.

¡Por aquí has de pasar,
corazón!
¡Por aquí,
corazón!

UNDERBRUSH

I stepped inside
the mortal hour.
Hour of the dying
and their last embrace.
A grave hour when
the captive bells are dreaming.

There are cuckoo-clocks,
but no cuckoo.
A mouldering star
and enormous pale
moths.

Amid the thicket
of sighs
I heard
the organ I used to hear
when I was a child.

Through here, my heart,
through here!
You must
come through here!

VISTA GENERAL

Toda la selva turbia
es una inmensa araña
que teje una red sonora
a la esperanza.
¡A la pobre virgen blanca
que se cría con suspiros y miradas!

GENERAL PROSPECT

The murky wood
is an enormous spider
spinning a resounding net
around hope.
A poor, white virgin
raised on sighs and longing looks!

ÉL

La verdadera esfinge
es el reloj.
Edipo nacerá de una pupila.
Limita al Norte
con el espejo
y al Sur
con el gato.
Doña Luna es una Venus.
(Esfera sin sabor.)
Los relojes nos traen
los inviernos.
(Golondrinas hieráticas
emigran el verano.)
La madrugada tiene
un pleamar de relojes
donde se ahoga el sueño.
Los murciélagos nacen
de las esferas
y el becerro los estudia
preocupado.
¿Cuándo será el crepúsuclo
de todos los relojes?
¿Cuándo esas lunas blancas
se hundirán por los montes?

HIM

The real sphynx
is the clock.
Oedipus will spring from one of its pupils.
It borders on the North
with the looking-glass
and to the South
with the cat.
Lady Moon is a Venus.
(Insipid sphere.)
Clocks bring us
winter.
(Hieratic swallows
migrate in summer.)
The dawn has a
high tide of clocks
where dreams are drowned.
Bats are born
of the spheres
and the heifer studies them
with some concern.
When will the twilight
of all clocks occur?
When will those white moons
go down along the mountains?

ECO DE RELOJ

Me senté
en un claro del tiempo.
Era un remanso de silencio,
de un blanco
silencio.
Anillo formidable
donde los luceros
chocaban con los doce flotantes
números negros.

MEDITACIÓN PRIMERA Y ÚLTIMA

El Tiempo
tiene color de noche.
De una noche quieta.
Sobre lunas enormes,
la Eternidad
está fija en las doce.
Y el Tiempo se ha dormido
para siempre en su torre.
Nos engañan
todos los relojes.
El Tiempo tiene ya
horizontes.

A CLOCK'S ECHO

I sat down
in a pause in time.
It was a pool of silence,
of white
silence.
A formidable ring
where the stars
bumped into
twelve floating black numerals.

FIRST AND LAST MEDITATION

Time the colour
of night.
Of a still night.
On enormous mirrors
Eternity
is stuck at twelve.
And Time has nodded off
forever in his tower.
All clocks
deceive us.
Time already
has horizons in sight.

LA HORA ESFINGE

En tu jardín se abren
las estrellas malditas.
Nacemos bajos tus cuernos
y morimos.
¡Hora fría!
Pones un techo de piedra
a las mariposas líricas
y, sentada en el azul,
cortas alas
y límites.

[UNA … DOS … Y TRES]

Una … dos … y tres.
Sonó la hora en la selva.
El silencio
se llenó de burbujas
y en péndulo de oro
llevaba y traía
mi cara por el aire.
¡Sonó la hora en la selva!
Los relojes de bolsillo,
como bandadas de moscas,
iban y venían.

En mi corazón sonaba
el reloj sobredorado
de mi abuelita.

SPHYNX TIME

Damnable stars
bloom in your garden.
We are born beneath your horns
and there we die.
The cold hour!
You set a roof of stone
over poetry's butterflies
and, sitting in the blue,
you clip wings
and audacity.

[ONE … TWO … THREE]

One … two … three.
The clock struck in the forest.
The silence
filled with bubbles
and my face
went swinging to and fro
on a pendulum of gold.
The clock struck in the forest!
Pocket watches
flew back and forth
like busy bands of flies.

In my heart Grandmother's
gilded clock.
was chiming.

CRUZ

CROSS

NORTE

Las estrellas frías
sobre los caminos.
Hay quien va y quien viene
por selvas de humo.
Los caballos suspiran
bajo la aurora perpetua.
¡En el golpe
del hacha
valles y bosques tienen
un temblor de cisterna!
¡En el golpe
del hacha!

SUR

Sur,
espejismo,
reflejo.
Da lo mismo decir
estrella que naranja,
cauce que cielo.

NORTH

Cold stars
above the roads.
In woods of smoke,
movement to and fro.
The cabins sigh
beneath the perpetual dawn.
With the blow of an axe
woods and valleys
shake like a cistern!
With the blow
of an axe!

SOUTH

South,
a mirage,
a reflection.
It's all the same
to say orange or star,
riverbed or sky.

¡Oh la flecha,
la flecha!
El Sur
es eso:
una flecha de oro,
¡sin blanco! sobre el viento.

ESTE

Escala de aroma
que baja
al Sur
(por grados conjuntos).

OESTE

Escala de luna
que asciende
al Norte
(cromática).

Oh, the arrow,
the arrow!
That is what
the South is:
an arrow of gold –
without target! –
in the wind.

EAST

A scale of fragrance
that goes down
South
(by degrees).

WEST

A scale of moonlight
that goes up
North
(chromatically).

SUITE DEL AGUA

WATER SUITE

PAÍS

En el agua negra,
árboles yacentes,
margaritas
y amapolas.

Por el camino muerto
van tres bueyes.

Por el aire,
el ruiseñor,
corazón del árbol.

TEMBLOR

En mi memoria turbia
con un recuerdo de plata,
piedra de rocío.

En el campo sin monte,
una laguna clara,
manantial apagado.

COUNTRY

Toppled trees,
poppies
and yellow-eyed daisies
on the black water.

Three oxen treading
the still road

In the air,
the nightingale,
heart of the tree.

TREMOR

In my muddied memory,
a silver reminiscence,
a stone of dew.

In fields without underbrush,
a clear lagoon,
an extinguished spring.

ACACIA

¿Quién segó el tallo
de la luna?

(Nos dejó raíces
de agua.)

¡Qué fácil nos sería cortar las flores
de la eterna acacia!

CURVA

Con un lirio en la mano
te dejo.
¡Amor de mi noche!
Y viudita de mi astro
te encuentro.

Domador de sombrías
mariposas,
sigo por mi camino.
Al cabo de mil años
me verás.
¡Amor de mi noche!
Por la vereda azul,
domador de sombrías
estrellas,
seguiré mi camino.
Hasta que el Universo
quepa en mi corazón.

ACACIA

Who has cut off
the stem of the moon?

(They left us
roots of water.)

How simple it would be to cut the flowers
of the eternal acacia!

CURVE

With an iris in my hand,
I leave you.
Love of my night!
And little widow of my star,
I find you.

I go my own way,
a tamer of
sombre butterflies.
When a thousand years have passed,
you will see me.
Love of my night!
Down the blue path
I go,
a tamer of
sombre stars.
Until the Universe
fits inside my heart.

COLMENA

¡Vivimos en celdas
de cristal,
en colmena de aire!
Nos besamos a través
de cristal.
¡Maravillosa cárcel,
cuya puerta es la luna!

BEEHIVE

We live in cells
of glass, in
a beehive of air!
We kiss
through panes of glass.
A marvellous jail,
whose gateway is the moon!

TRES CREPÚSCULOS

A Conchita, mi hermana

THREE TWILIGHTS

For my sister, Conchita

I

La tarde está
arrepentida
porque sueña
con el mediodía.
(Árboles rojos y nubes
sobre las colinas.)
La tarde soltó su verde
caballera lírica
y tiembla dulcemente
…le fastidia
ser tarde habiendo sido
mediodía.

II

¡Ahora empieza la tarde!
¿Por qué? ¿Por qué?
…Ahora mismo
he visto al día inclinarse
como un lirio.
La flor de la mañana
dobla el tallo
…ahora mismo…
La raíz de la tarde
surge de lo sombrío.

I

The afternoon
is full of rue,
because it dreams
it was high noon.
(Red trees and clouds
above the hill.)
Evening shakes out
its lyrical green mane
and trembles without a sound.
…Unhappy to be afternoon
when once it was
high noon.

II

Now evening begins!
(Why is that? Why?)
…Just now
I have seen the day
drooping like a lily.
The flower of the morning
doubled over on its stem,
…just now…
The root of evening
shoots up from the shadows.

III

¡Adiós, sol!

Bien sé que eres la luna,
pero yo
no lo diré a nadie,
sol.
Te ocultas
detrás del telón
y disfrazas tu rostro
con polvos de arroz.
De día, la guitarra
del labrador;
de noche, la mandolina
de Pierrot.
¡Qué más da!
Tu ilusión
es crear el jardín
multicolor.
¡Adiós, sol!
No olvides lo que te ama
el caracol,
la viejecilla del balcón,
y yo…
que juego al trompo con mi…
corazón.

III

So long, sun!
I know you are the moon
but I
won't tell.
You hide
behind the curtain
and mask your face
in rice powder.
By day a farmhand's
guitar.
By night Pierrot's
mandolin.
What matter!
You dream you can create
the garden of many colours.
Good-bye, sun!
Don't forget
how much the snail,
the old lady
on her balcony,
and I…,
who play
with the spinning top
of my heart,
love you.

PAÍSES

COUNTRIES

NIEVE

Campo sin caminos
y ciudad sin tejados.
El mundo está silencioso
y cándido.

Paloma gigantesca
de los astros,
¿cómo no baja del azul
el eterno milano?

MUNDO

Ángulo eterno,
la tierra y el cielo.
Con bisectriz de viento.

Ángulo inmenso,
el camino derecho.
Con bisectriz de deseo.

Las paralelas se encuentran
en el beso.
¡Oh corazón
sin eco!
En ti empieza y acaba
el universo.

SNOW

Country without a track
and city without a roof.
The world is silent
and immaculately white.

Tell me, great dove
of the heavenly bodies,
how is it the eternal hawk
does not drop from the blue?

WORLD

Earth and sky,
in an eternal angle.
Bisected by the wind.

The road straight ahead
is an immense angle,
bisected by desire.

Parallel lines
meet in a kiss.
Oh heart
without echo!
The universe begins and ends
in you.

HISTORIETAS DEL VIENTO

LITTLE STORIES OF THE WIND

I

El viento venía rojo
por el collado encendido
y se ha puesto verde, verde
por el río.
Luego se pondrá violeta,
amarillo y…
será sobre los sembrados
un arco iris tendido.

II

Viento estancado.
Arriba el sol.
Abajo
las algas temblorosas
de los álamos.
Y mi corazón
temblando.
Viento estancado
a las cinco de la tarde
sin pájaros.

I

The wind blew red
down the sunlit hill
and went dark green
by the river.
Later it will go
all violet and yellow…
and arch like a rainbow
over new-sown fields.

II

Wind at a stand-still.
Overhead the sun.
Below,
the aspens'
trembling algae.
And my heart, as well,
atremble.
Wind at a stand-still
at five in the afternoon,
not a bird to be seen.

III

La brisa
es ondulada
como los cabellos
de algunas muchachas.
Como los marecitos
de algunas viejas tablas.
La brisa
brota como el agua,
y se derrama
– tenue bálsamo blanco –
por las cañadas,
y se desmaya
al chocar con lo duro
de la montaña.

ROSA

¡Rosa de los vientos!
(Metamorfosis
del punto negro.)
¡Rosa de los vientos!
Punto florecido.
Punto abierto.

III

The breeze
comes in waves
like some girls'
tresses.
Like some little seas
in certain old paintings.
The breeze
bubbles like water
and spills
over and down the gullies
– a thin white balsam –
falling in a faint,
in a head-on collision
with the mountain's hard face.

ROSE

Rose of the four winds!
(Metamorphosis
of the black compass point.)
Rose of the winds!
(A point in bloom,
a full-blown point.)

ESCUELA

Maestro
¡Qué doncella se casa
con el viento?

Niño
La doncella de todos
los deseos.

Maestro
¿Qué le regala
el viento?

Niño
Remolinos de oro
y mapas superpuestos.

Maestro
¿Ella le ofrece algo?

Niño
Su corazón abierto.

Maestro
Decid como se llama.

Niño
Su nombre es un secreto.

(La ventana
del colegio
tiene una cortina
de luceros.)

SCHOOL

Teacher
  Which young lady will wed the wind?

Little boy
  The lady all long for.

Teacher
  What will the wind give her?

Little boy
  Pin-wheels of gold
  and maps, one atop the other.

Teacher
  And does she have something for him?

Little boy
  Her unlocked heart.

Teacher
  Tell me her name.

Little boy
  Her name is a secret.

(The window
 in the school
has a curtain
of evening stars.)

ENSUEÑOS DEL RÍO

Río Genil

RIVERSIDE REVERIES

Genil River

Las alamedas se van,
pero dejan su reflejo.

   (¡Oh qué bello
   momento!)

Las alamedas se van,
pero nos dejan el viento.

El viento está amortajado
a lo largo, bajo el cielo.

   (¡Oh qué triste
   momento!)

Pero ha dejado flotando,
sobre los ríos, sus ecos.

El mundo de las luciérnagas
ha invadido mis recuerdos.

   (¡Oh qué bello
   momento!)

Y un corazón diminuto
me va brotando en los dedos.

The poplars are fading
but their reflection lingers.

  (Oh what a beautiful
  moment!)

The poplars are fading
but the wind lingers.

Below the sky the wind is
in a shroud, all along the river.

  (Oh what a sad
  moment!)

But its echoes linger,
afloat on the river.

The world of fireflies
has invaded my memory.

  (Oh what a beautiful
  moment!)

And a little heart
buds in my fingers.

[EL REMANSO TIENE LOTOS]

El remanso tiene lotos
de círculos concéntricos.
Sobre mis sienes soporto
la majestad del silencio.

Maravillosos biseles
estremecen a los álamos.
Por las hierbas de la orilla
van los caracoles blancos.

CORRIENTE LENTA

En el Cubillas

Por el río se van mis ojos,
por el río…

Por el río se va mi amor,
por el río…

(Mi corazón va contando
las horas que está dormido.)

El río trae hojas secas,
el río…

El río es claro y profundo,
el río…

(Mi corazón me pregunta
si puede cambiar de sitio.)

[LOTUSES IN CONCENTRIC CIRCLES]

Lotuses in concentric circles
on the still water.
On my temples I bear
the majesty of silence.

Marvellous bevels
send a shiver through the poplars.
White snails climb
grasses on the bank.

LAZY CURRENT

On the Cubillas River

Down the river go my eyes,
down the river…

Down the river goes my love,
down the river…

(My heart is counting the hours
it has been asleep.)

The river has dead leaves in it,
the river…

The river is clear and deep,
the river…

(My heart is asking
if it can be somewhere else.)

MADRIGALS

MADRIGALS

I

Como las ondas concéntricas
sobre el agua,
así en el corazón
tus palabras.

Como un pájaro que choca
con el viento,
así sobre mis labios
tus besos.

Como fuentes abiertas
frente a la tarde,
así mis ojos negros
sobre tu carne.

I

Like concentric waves
on the water,
just so, your words
in my heart.

Like a bird crashing
into the wind.
Just so, your kisses
on my lips.

Like opened fountains
facing the night,
just so, my jet-black eyes
on your flesh.

II

Estoy preso
en tus círculos
concéntricos.
¡Como Saturno
llevo
los anillos
de mi sueño!
Y no acabo de hundirme
ni me elevo.
¡Amor mío!
Mi cuerpo
flota sobre el remanso
de los besos.

II

I am prisoner
of your concentric
circles.
Like Saturn
I wear
the rings
of my dream.
And I can't quite sink
nor can I rise up.
My love!
My body floats
on the still water
of your kisses.

CASTILLO DE FUEGOS ARTIFICIALES QUEMADO CON MOTIVO DEL CUMPLEAÑOS DEL POETA

CASTLE OF FIREWORKS DISPLAYED ON THE POET'S BIRTHDAY

PRIMERA COHETERÍA

Tú tú tú tú
yo yo yo yo.
¿Quién?...
¡ni tú
ni yo!

RUEDA CATALINA

Doña Catalina
tenía un pelo de oro
entre su cabellera
de sombra.

(¿A quién espero,
Dios mío,
a quién espero?)

Doña Catalina
camina despacio
poniendo estrellitas
verdes en la noche.

(Ni aquí
ni allí
sino aquí.)

Doña Catalina
se muere y le nace
una granadeta de luz
en la frente.

¡Chissssssssssssssssss!

FIRST ROUND OF ROCKETS

You-you-you-you
I-I-I-I
Who?
Neither you
nor I!

CATHERINE WHEEL

Dame Catherine
had one golden hair
in the middle
of her shadowy tresses.

(Who am I waiting for,
dear God,
who am I waiting for?)

Dame Catherine
proceeds slowly,
hanging little green stars
in the night.

(Neither here
nor there
but here.)

Dame Catherine
is dying and a little
grenade of light
breaks over her brow.

Chisssssssssssssssssss!

COHETES

Seis lanzas de fuego
suben.
(La noche es una guitarra.)
Seis sierpes enfurecidas.
(Por el cielo vendrá San Jorge.)
Seis sopletes de oro y viento.
(¿Se agrandará la ampolla de la noche?)

JARDÍN CHINO

En bosquecillos
de grana y magnesio
saltan las princesitas.
Chispas.

Hay una lluvia de naranjas
sobre el zig-zag de los cerezos
y entre comas vuelan azules
dragoncillos amaestrados.

Niña mía, este jardincillo
es para verlo en los espejitos
de tus uñas.
Para verlo en el biombo
de tus dientes.
Y ser como un ratoncito.

ROCKETS

Six fiery lances
lift off.
(The night is a guitar.)
Six infuriated serpents.
(St George will come through the sky.)
Six torches of gold and wind.
(Will the jar of the night
grow bigger?)

LITTLE CHINESE GARDEN

In little woods
of crimson and magnesium
princesses jump.
Sparks.

There is a rain of oranges
over zigzagging cherry trees
and tame blue dragons
fly amid commas.

Little girl, this tiny garden
is for you to see in the glass
of your fingernails.
For you to see on the screen
of your little white teeth.
And to be like a little mouse.

GIRASOL

Si yo amara a un cíclope
suspiraría
bajo esta mirada
sin párpados.
¡Oh girasol de fuego!
El gentío lo mira
sin estremecimiento.
¡Ojo de la providencia
ante una muchedumbre
de Abeles!

¡Girasol girasol!
¡Ojo salvaje y puro
sin la ironía del guiño!

¡Girasol girasol!
¡Estigma ardiente sobre
los gentíos de feria!

SUNFLOWER

If I were to love a Cyclops,
I would sigh
beneath this lidless
gaze.
Oh fiery sunflower!
The crowd looks on
unshuddering.
The eye of providence
trained on a multitude
of Abels!

Sunflower! Sunflower!
Eye savage and pure
without so much as the irony
of a wink!

Sunflower! Sunflower!
Burning stigma
on the people at the fair!

DISCO DE RUBÍES

Gira y se estremece
como loco.
No sabe nada
¿y lo sabe todo?
¡Todas las flechas
a este corazón
redondo!

Todas las pupilas
a este corazón
redondo.
¡Lupa sangrienta entre
el misterio
y nosotros!

RUBY DISK

It spins and it shakes
like mad.
It knows nothing and –
knows it all?
All arrows
to this round
heart!

All eyes
on this round
heart.
Red magnifying glass
between the mystery
and ourselves!

CAPRICHO

¡Tris!...
¿Has cerrado
los ojos?
¡Triis!...
¿Más aún? Será una
muchacha de brisa.
Yo soy un hombre.
¡Tras!...
Ya te vas, amor mío,
¿y tus ojos?
¡Traaas!...
Si los cierras, yo tengo dos plumas.
¿Lo oyes? Dos plumas que miran
de mi pavo real.
¡Tris!...
¿Me has oído?
¡Traaas!...

CAPRICCIO

Snip…!
Have you closed
your eyes?
S-nip…!
Even tighter? Must be
a girl of wind.
I am a man.
Snap…!
Already going, my love?
What about your eyes?
S-nap!...
If you close them, I've got two feathers,
do you hear? Two peacock feathers
with eyes that see.
Snip!
Did you hear what I said?
S-nap…!

JUEGO DE LUNAS

La luna esta redonda.
Alrededor, una noria
de espejos.
Alrededor, una rueda
de agua.
La luna se ha hecho láminas
como un pan de oro blanco.
La luna se ha deshojado
en lunas.
Bandadas de fuentes
vuelan por el aire.
En cada fuente yace
una luna difunta.
La luna
se hace un bastón de luz
en el torrente claro.
La luna
como una gran vidriera
rota, cae sobre el mar.
La luna
se va por un biombo
infinito.
¿Y la Luna? ¿Y la Luna?

(Arriba,
no queda más que un aro
de cristalillos.)

GAME OF MOONS

Round moon.
All about it, a wheel
of mirrors.
All about it, a water
wheel.
The moon's now a tissue
of white gold-leaf.
The moon has
peeled off
into moon-leaves.
Swarming fountains
fly through the air.
In every one lies
a different moon, defunct.
In the bright torrent
the moon becomes
a cane of light.
Like a big broken window
the moon
falls apart on the sea.
The moon
goes behind an endless
screen.
And the capital M Moon? What about her?

(Overhead there is
nothing but a hoop
of broken bits of glass.)

SURTIDORES

WATER JETS

INTERIOR

Desde mi cuarto
oigo el surtidor.
Un dedo de la parca
y un rayo de sol
señalan hacia el sitio
de mi corazón.
Por el aire de Agosto
se van las nubes; yo
sueño que no sueño
dentro del surtidor.

PAÍS

¡Surtidores de los sueños
sin aguas
y sin fuentes!

Se ven con el rabillo
del ojo, nunca frente
a frente.

Como todas las cosas
ideales, se mecen
en las márgenes puras
de la Muerte.

INTERIOR

From inside my room
I hear the fountain fall.
One finger of Fate
and a sunbeam
point to the place
my heart is.
Clouds drift
through the August air, I
dream I do not dream
inside the fountain.

COUNTRY

Dream fountains
without water
and without basin!

You see them from the corner
of your eye, never
face to face.

Like all ideal things,
they sway
on the pure margins
of Death.

APARTE

La sangre de la noche
va por las arterías
de los surtidores.
¡Oh qué maravilla
de temblor!
Yo pienso
en ventanas abiertas,
sin pianos
y sin doncellas.

[¡HACE UN INSTANTE!]

[…]
¡Hace un instante!
Todavía la polvareda
se mece en el azul.
¡Hace un momento!
¡Dos mil siglos!
si mal no recuerdo.

AN ASIDE

Blood of the night
runs through the fountains'
arteries.
Oh, what a marvellous
quaking!
I think of
open windows,
without pianos
and without maidens.

[AN INSTANT AGO!]

[…]
An instant ago!
The dust still
sways in the blue.
A moment ago!
Two thousand centuries!
If my memory serves me well.

JARDÍN

Hay cuatro caballeros
con espadas de agua
y está la noche oscura.
Las cuatro espadas hieren
el mundo de las rosas
y os herirán el corazón.
¡No bajéis al jardín!

GARDEN

There are four knights
with swords of water
and the night is dark.
Four swords to wound
the world of the roses.
And they shall wound your heart.
Don't go down to the garden!

HERBARIOS

HERBALS

LIBRO

I

El viajante de jardines
lleva un herbario.
Con su tomo de olor, gira.

Por las noches vienen a sus ramas
las almas de los viejos pájaros.

Cantan en ese bosque comprimido
Que requiere las fuentes del llanto.

Como las naricillas de los niños
aplastadas en el cristal opaco,
así las flores de este libro
sobre el cristal invisible de los años.

El viajante de jardines,
abre el libro llorando
y los olores errabundos
se desmayan sobre el herbario.

BOOK

I

The travelling salesman
is peddling gardens in an herbal;
a tome of perfume, whirling.

At night the souls of elderly birds
light on its branches.

They sing in a miniature wood
watered with tears.

Like the noses of little children
pressed on opaque glass,
so the flowers pressed
on the invisible glass of the years.

The salesman with gardens for sale
opens his book, weeping,
and wandering fragrances
fall in a faint on its pages.

II

El viajante del tiempo
trae el herbario de los sueños.

Yo
¿Dónde está el herbario?

El viajante
Lo tienes en tus manos.

Yo
Tengo libres los diez dedos.

El viajante
Los sueños bailan en tus cabellos.

Yo
¿Cuántos siglos han pasado?

El viajante
Una sola hoja
tiene mi herbario.

Yo
¿Voy al alba
o a la tarde?

El viajante
El pasado
está inhabitable.

Yo
¡Oh jardín de la amarga fruta!

El viajante
¡Peor es el herbario de la luna!

II

The salesman of time
is here with the herbal of dreams.

Me
Where is the herbal?

Salesman
You have it in your hands.

Me
All ten of my fingers are free.

Salesman
Dreams are dancing in your hair.

Me
How many centuries have passed?

Salesman
There is but one page in my herbal.

Me
Am I headed for dawn or dusk?

Salesman
The past is uninhabitable.

Me
Oh garden of bitter fruit!

Salesman
Far worse is the herbal of the moon!

III

En mucho secreto, un amigo
me enseña el herbario de los ruidos.

(¡Chisss… silencio!
La noche cuelga del cielo.)

A la luz de un puerto perdido
vienen los ecos de todos los siglos.

(¡Chisss… silencio!
¡La noche oscila con el viento!)
(¡Chisss… silencio!
Viejas iras se enroscan en mis dedos.)

III

In great secrecy, a friend
shows me the herbal of sounds.

(Sh–h–h! Quiet!
Night hangs from the sky.)

By the light of a lost mountain pass
come the echoes of all the centuries.

(Sh–h–h!... Quiet!
The wind unsteadies the night.)
(Sh–h–h!… Quiet!
Old resentments twine about my fingers.)

CARACOL

SNAIL

CARACOL

Caracol,
estáte quieto.

Donde tú estés
estará el centro.

La piedra sobre el agua
y el grito en el viento
forman las imágenes
puras de tu ensueño.
Las circunferencias
imposibles en tu cuerpo.

Caracol, col, col, col,
estáte quieto.

Donde tú estés
estará el centro.

SNAIL

Little snail,
be still.

Wherever you are
there will be the centre.

A stone skipping over the water
and a cry borne on the wind
figure the pure
images of your dream.
The impossible
circumferences of your body.

Little snail, little snail,
be still.

Wherever you are
there will be the centre.

ESPIRAL

Mi tiempo
avanza en espiral.

La espiral
limita mi paisaje,
deja en tinieblas lo pasado
y me hace caminar
lleno de incertidumbre.

¡Oh línea recta! Pura
lanza sin caballero.

¡Cómo sueña tu luz
mi senda salomónica!

SPIRAL

My time
moves in a spiral.

The spiral delimits
what I see.
It leaves the past in darkness.
Makes me walk
full of uncertainty.

Oh arrow-straight line!
Lance without a knight.

How my meandering way
dreams of your light!

BALADA DEL CARACOL BLANCO

Caracoles blancos.
Los niños juegan
bajo los álamos.
El río viejecito
va muy despacio
sentándose en las sillas
verdes de los remansos.
Mi niño, ¿dónde está?
Quiere ser un caballo
¡tilín! ¡tilín! ¡tilin! Mi niño
¡qué loquillo! cantando
quiere salirse
de mi corazón cerrado.

Caracolitos chicos.
Caracoles blancos.

BALLAD OF THE WHITE SNAIL

White snails.
The children play
beneath the poplars.
The little old river
moves very slowly,
pausing to sit
on green chairs of pooling water.
My little boy, where is he?
He wants to be a horse.
Jingle-jangle! My little boy
is a mad little thing! He sings,
he wants to break out
of my locked-up heart.

Tiny little snails,
little white snails.

BALADA DEL CARACOL NEGRO

Caracoles negros.
Los niños sentados
escuchan un cuento.
El río traía
coronas de viento
y una gran serpiente
desde un tronco viejo
miraba las nubes
redondas del cielo.
Niño mío chico
¿dónde estás?
Te siento
en el corazón
y no es verdad. Lejos
esperas que yo saque
tu alma del silencio.

Caracoles grandes.
Caracoles negros.

BALLAD OF THE BLACK SNAIL

Black snails.
The children sit
listening to a story.
The river brought
wreaths of wind
and on an old tree-trunk
a great big snake
gazed at the round
clouds in the sky.
My little boy, little one,
where are you? I feel you
in my heart
and it isn't so! From far away
you wait for me
to pluck your soul
from the silence.

Great big snails.
Black snails.

EN EL BOSQUE DE LAS TORONJAS DE LUNA

Poema extático

IN THE WOOD OF THE LUNAR GRAPEFRUITS

An ecstatic poem

PRÓLOGO

Me voy a un largo viaje.

Sobre un espejo de plata encuentro, mucho antes de que amanezca, el maletín y la ropa que debo usar por las extrañísimas tierras y jardines teóricos.

Pobre y tranquilo, quiero visitar el mundo extático donde viven todas mis posibilidades y paisajes perdidos. Quiero entrar frío y agudo en el jardín de las simientes no florecidas y de las teorías ciegas, en busca del amor que no tuve pero que era mío.

He buscado durante largos días por todos los espejos de mi casa el camino que conduce a ese jardín maravilloso y al fin, ¡por pura casualidad!, lo he encontrado.

Adopté muchos procedimientos. Por ejemplo, me puse a cantar procurando que mi voz se mantuviera larga y tensa sobre el aire, pero los espejos permanecían silenciosos. Hice complicadas geometrías con la palabra y el ritmo, llené los ojos de plata con mi llanto y hasta puse una pantalla a la lamparita que ilumina la gruta de mi cabeza, ¡pero todo fue inútil!

Una mañana velada, después que había desechado por imposible el proyecto de viaje y me hallaba libre de preocupaciones y de jardines invisibles, fui a peinarme ante un espejo y, sin preguntarle nada, su ancha cara de plata se llenó de un zigzag de cantos de ruiseñores, y en la profundidad del azogue surgió la clave clara y precisa, clave que naturalmente me está vedado revelar.

Yo emprendo sereno este viaje y desde luego me lavo las manos: contaré lo que vea, pero no me pidáis que explique nada.

Pude haber ido al país de los muertos pero prefiero ir al país de lo que no vive, que no es lo mismo.

Desde luego que un alma *pura y completa* no sentirá esta curiosidad. Voy tranquilo. En el maletín llevo una buena provisión de luciérnagas.

*

Antes de marchar siento un dolor agudo en el corazón. Mi familia duerme y toda la casa está en un reposo absoluto. El alba revelando torres y contando una a una las hojas de los árboles me pone un antifaz blanco y unos guantes de [?]

PROLOGUE

I am going away on a long journey.

In a looking-glass of silver, well before the break of dawn, I find the satchel and the clothing that I am going to use for travel in strange lands and theoretical gardens.

Poor but at peace with myself, I want to visit the ecstatic world where all my possibilities and lost landscapes live. I want to enter, cool but sharp-witted, into the garden of blind theories and seeds that did not flower, in search of the love that I never had but was mine.

For days on end I have looked in every mirror in my house for the road that leads to that marvellous garden and at last – by sheer chance! – I have found it.

I tried many ploys. For example, I began to sing, trying to keep my voice long and tense in the air, but the mirrors remained silent. I performed complicated geometries with words and rhythm, I filled silvery eyes with my lament, and I even placed a shade around the little lamp that lights the grotto in my head, but to no avail.

One dim morning, after I had given up on the idea of a journey and I was feeling free of all concern for invisible gardens, I went to comb my hair in front of the mirror and, without my asking anything of it, its broad silver face broke into a zigzag of nightingales' song, and in the depths of the mercury the secret key appeared, clear and precise, the key that, naturally, I am not allowed to reveal.

I am setting out on this journey in a serene frame of mind and, needless to say, I am washing my hands of it. I will tell you what I see, but don't ask me to explain anything about it.

I could have gone to the country of the dead but I prefer to go to the country of what is not alive, which is not the same thing.

To be sure, a *pure and complete* soul would not feel this curiosity. I am not worried. In my satchel I am carrying a good supply of fireflies.

Before going out the door I feel a sharp pain in my heart. My family is sleeping and the entire house is in absolute repose. Dawn begins to reveal towers and counting the leaves on the trees one by one it places a white mask on me and gloves of [text breaks off]

REFLEXIÓN

Hombre que vas y vienes,
huye del río y el viento,
cierra los ojos y…
…y vendimia tus lágrimas.

Con el alma en un hilo,
olvida la pregunta.
No menees las hoces
de la interrogación.

La pregunta es la yedra
que nos cubre y despista.
Giran ante nuestros ojos
prismas y encrucijadas.

La pregunta es la misma
pregunta disfrazada.
Va como manantial
y vuelve como espejo.

[…]

REFLECTION

You who come and go,
run from the river and wind,
close your eyes and…
…harvest your tears.

Soul hanging by a thread,
never mind the question.
Do not rattle the sickles
of interrogation.

The question is the ivy
that covers and throws us off.
Prisms and crossroads
whirl before our eyes.

The answer is the same as
the question, in disguise.
It starts out as a spring
and comes back as a mirror.

[…]

LAS TRES BRUJAS DESENGAÑADORAS

En la puerta del jardín

Bruja 1ª
¡Ay flauta del sapo
y luz del gusano!

2ª.
¡Ay mares de fósforo
y bosques de acero!

3ª.
Nuestra enemiga la blanca
luz de los siete colores.

1ª.
Mis lágrimas darán el arco
negro de la luz negra.

2ª.
Vuelvan las cosas, vuelvan
a sus primeros planos.

3ª.
Reino de la semilla
y la tiniebla extática.

2ª.
Mundo sin ojos, mundo
sin laberinto, ni reflejo.

THE THREE UNDECEIVING WITCHES

At the door of the garden

Witch No. 1
Woe the toad's flute
and the worm's light!

Witch No. 2
Woe seas of phosphorus
and woodlands of steel!

Witch No. 3
Our enemy is white light
with its seven colours.

No. 1
My tears will yield
the rainbow of black light.

No. 2
Let things go back, back
to their foreworld.

No. 3
The kingdom of the seed
and ecstatic gloom.

No. 2
World without eyes, without
labyrinths or reflection.

3ª.
Teorías. Altas torres
sin cimientos ni piedras.

1ª.
Flauta del sapo.
Luz del gusano.

Las tres
Cada cosa en su círculo.
Todos desconocidos.
El viento no contesta
las preguntas del árbol.

3ª.
¡Reino de la semilla
y la tiniebla extática!

2ª.
¡Ah flor equivocada
sobre el tallo ignorante!

1ª.
Hermanas, cegad las siete
pupilas del dragón blanco.

Las tres
Cada cosa en su círculo.
Todos desconocidos.
Cansadas estamos, ¡bizcas!
de ir por el mismo sitio.

***

No. 3
Theories. High towers
without foundation or stones.

No. 1
Toad flute.
Worm light.

All three
Let everything stay in its circle.
Each unrecognizable to each.
The wind does not answer
questions from the tree.

No. 3
The kingdom of the seed
and ecstatic gloom!

No. 2

Woe the wayward flower
on the unsuspecting stem!

No. 1
Sisters, blind the seven pupils
of the white dragon's eyes.

All three
Let everything remain as it was.
Each unrecognizable to each.
We are weary – we are squint-eyed! –
from going round in circles

[…]
(Detrás de la puerta ríen
dos calaveras con alas.)

  ¿Quién es?

Voy al bosque inexpugnable
de las toronjas de luna.

Traga o escupe el bocado
de Adán.
  Se ha deshojado la puerta.
Tres anchas risas, sin dientes,
devoran mi fresca risa.
  […]

[…]
(Behind the door two skulls
with wings guffaw.)

   Who's there?

I'm going to the unassailable wood
of lunar grapefruits.

Swallow or spit out
the mouthful Adam took.
   The door has come off its hinges.
Three broad, toothless guffaws
devour my young man's mirth.
[…]

SITUACIÓN

La primera sierpe de viento
va entre alamedas sin savia.

Yo tengo una larga barba
de padre río.

Recuerdo viejas muchedumbres,
noches ciegas y pájaros sonámbulos.
Mi siglo como un río de agua gris
y mi laúd con las velas de plomo.

¡Qué cansancio de cielos en mis ojos!
Un calambre de alba permanente
aprisiona mi carne envejecida
con sus ramajes yertos y agitados.

　Tan-tan
(Se iba la Tierra empedrada de cúpulas
bajo la cáscara azul de la atmósfera.)

　¿Quién es?

(Entre una luz de leche y de luna
llego a la torre donde ya me esperan.)

SITUATION

The first snake of wind
moves amid sapless poplars.

I have a long beard
like old man river.

I remember old crowds,
blind nights and sleepwalking birds.
My century is like a grey river
and my boat has sails of lead.

What a tedium of skies in my eyes!
Dawn's perennial cramp
imprisons my aging flesh
with its stiff and shaking trees.

Knock-knock
(The Earth was moving away, paved with domes,
beneath the blue eggshell of the atmosphere.)

Who's there?

(Between milk and moonlight
I arrive at the tower where already they await me.)

TORRE

Él estaba
con su corona
de carcajadas.
Larga barba amarilla.

Él
Te esperaba.

Yo
La ganzúa del Sueño
me abrió su mansión.
        Vive
lo que no vivió nunca
ni vivirá. Mis ojos,
llenos de escarcha, copian
blancos bosques inmóviles.

Él
Dentro de cada estrella
hay un gusano de oro.
El dragón oculta una risa
de niño bajo un ala.

Yo
¡Ah bribón! ¡gran bribón!
Nada puedo ofrecerte
¡Ni risa ni gusano!

Él
Señor, tienes cien años.

TOWER

He was there
with his crown
of loud guffaws.
A long yellow beard.

Him
I was waiting for you.

Me
The skeleton key of the Dreamworld
opened its mansion to me.
What never lived nor will live
        is alive.
My eyes, full of frost, copy
motionless white woods.

Him
Inside of every star
is a golden worm.
The dragon hides a child's
laughter beneath its wing.

Me
Scoundrel! You scoundrel!
I have nothing to offer you.
Neither laughter nor worm!

Him
Sir, you are a hundred years old.

Yo
Cien no, sobre los hombros
cada año una espada
larga de luz undosa.

Él
¿Cómo pasaste el río
de mariposas de agua?

Yo
Con la ganzúa del Sueño
y a pesar tuyo.

Él
   Dame
tus labios.

Yo
   ¡Imposible!
¿Mi jardín de palabras?

Él
¿Tiemblas? Mira tu mundo.

Las Campanas (a lo lejos)
         Tin tan
         Tin Tan

¡Ah Navidad en tu casa!
La luna daba turquesas
a los ritmos de hojalata.
Aquel nacía de barro.
¡Ah Navidad de tu casa!

Me
No, not a hundred. On my shoulders
for every year there is
a long sword of waving light.

Him
How did you ford the river
of watery butterflies?

*M*e
With the skeleton key of the Dreamworld
and despite you.

Him
  Give me
your lips.

Me
  That's out of the question!
My garden of words?

Him
Do you tremble? Behold your world.

The Bells (from far away)
        Ding dong
        Ding dong

Oh Christmas in your home!
The moon lent turquoise
to the tinpan rhythms.
He was born of clay.
Oh Christmas in your home!

Nosotras te veíamos
sin corazón y sin cara
hacer puentes y látigos
grises con tu alma.

      Tin tan
      Tin tan

¡Adiós! ¡adiós! Y Memento,
¡pobre luz descarriada!
Gigantes nardos de tiniebla
rodean tu vieja casa.

      Tin tan
      Tin tan

Él
Alma tullida pero cristalina,
¡mira el jardín!

Los viejos plenilunios
como discos inmensos de cristal
brillaban apoyados en la fronda.

Las Campanas de la Torre (solas)
      ¡Ah ¡Ah!

¿Cuándo dormiremos?
La sombra pesa sobre
nuestros ojos sin párpados.
¿Cuándo dormiremos?
Cortar nuestra flor
o darnos escafandra.

      ¡Ah! ¡Ah!

We all saw you
without a heart and without a face,
making bridges and
grey whips with your soul.

> Ding dong
> Ding dong

Farewell, farewell and remember,
poor little light gone astray!
Gigantic spikenards of gloom
surround your old home.

> Ding dong
> Ding dong

Him
Soul, crippled but crystal-clear,
behold your garden!

The old full moons
shone against the leaves on the trees
like immense crystal disks.

The Bells in the Tower (by themselves)
> Oh! Oh!

When will we sleep?
Shadow weighs heavy on
our lidless eyes.
When will we sleep?
Cut away our flower
or give us a diving-suit.

> Oh! Oh!

EN EL JARDÍN DE LAS TORONJAS DE LUNA

IN THE GARDEN OF THE LUNAR GRAPEFRUITS

PRÓLOGO

Asy como la sombra nuestra vida se va,
Que nunca más torna nyn de nos tornará
Pero López de Ayala, *Consejos morales*

Me he despedido de los amigos que más quiero para emprender un corto pero dramático viaje. Sobre un espejo de plata encuentro, mucho antes de que amanezca, el maletín con la ropa que debo usar en la extraña tierra a que me dirijo.

El perfume tenso y frío de la madrugada bate misteriosamente el inmenso acantilado de la noche.

En la página tersa del cielo temblaba la inicial de una nube, y debajo de mi balcón un ruiseñor y una rana levantan en el aire un aspa soñolienta de sonido.

Yo, tranquilo pero melancólico, hago los últimos preparativos, embargado por sutilísimas emociones de alas y círculos concéntricos. Sobre la blanca pared del cuarto, yerta y rígida como una serpiente de museo, cuelga la espada gloriosa que llevó mi abuelo en la guerra contra el rey don Carlos de Borbón.

Piadosamente descuelgo esa espada, vestida de herrumbre amarillenta como un álamo blanco, y me la ciño recordando que tengo que sostener una gran lucha invisible antes de entrar en el jardín. Lucha extática y violentísima con mi enemigo secular, el gigantesco dragón del Sentido Común.

Una emoción aguda y elegíaca por las cosas que no han sido, buenas y malas, grandes y pequeñas, invade los paisajes de mis ojos casi ocultos por unas gafas de luz violeta. Una emoción amarga me hace caminar hasta este jardín que se estremece en las altísimas llanuras del aire.

Los ojos de todas las criaturas golpean como puntos fosfóricos sobre la pared del porvenir…lo de atrás se queda lleno de maleza amarilla, huertos sin frutos y ríos sin agua. Jamás ningún hombre cayó de espaldas sobre la muerte. Pero yo, por un momento, contemplando ese paisaje abandonado e infinito, he visto planos de vida inédita, múltiples y superpuestos como los cangilones de una noria sin fin.

PROLOGUE

Like a shadow our life goes by,
never to come back nor from us return.

Pero López de Ayala, *Moral counsel*

I have said goodbye to my dearest friends in order to set out on a short but dramatic journey. Well before dawn, on a looking-glass of silver, I find the satchel with the clothes I am going to need in the strange land where I am bound.

The stiff, cold perfume of early morning beats mysteriously on the immense cliff of the night.

The initial of a cloud trembled on the smooth page of the sky, and under my balcony a nightingale and a frog raise a sleepy arm of sound.

Calmly but with melancholy, I make the final preparations. I am overwhelmed by the subtlest emotions of wings and concentric circles. On the white wall of the room, [as] stiff and rigid as a snake in a museum, hangs the glorious sword my grandfather used in the war against King Carlos the Pretender.

I take the sword down reverently; it wears a mantle of yellow rust like a white poplar, and I fasten it to my waist, bearing in mind that I must wage a great invisible battle before entering the garden. An ecstatic and fierce struggle with my enemy from time immemorial, the giant dragon of Common Sense.

A sharp and elegiac feeling for things that have not been, both good and bad, big and small, invades the landscapes in my eyes, all but hidden by violet-light glasses. A bitter feeling that compels me to walk toward this garden that shimmers on the high plains of the air.

The eyes of all creatures beat like phosphorescent points on the wall of the future … what lies behind is full of yellow scrub, of orchards without fruit and rivers without water. No man has ever fallen backwards into death. But I, for a moment, gazing on that infinite and desert landscape, have seen life's unheard-of blueprints, multiplied and superimposed atop one another like the buckets of a water-wheel without end.

Antes de marchar siento un dolor agudo en el corazón. Mi familia duerme y toda la casa está en un reposo absoluto. El alba, revelando torres y contando una a una las hojas de los árboles, me pone un crujiente vestido de encaje lumínico.

Algo se me olvida … no me cabe la menor duda … ¡tanto tiempo preparándome! Y … Señor, ¿qué se me olvida? ¡Ah! Un pedazo de madera … uno bueno de cerezo sonrosado y compacto.

Creo que hay que ir bien presentado…De una jarra con flores puesta sobre mi mesilla me prendo en el ojal siniestro una gran rosa pálida que tiene un rostro enfurecido pero hierático.

Ya es la hora.

(En las bandejas irregulares de las campanadas, vienen los kirikis de los gallos.)

Before I go I feel a sharp pain in my heart. My family is asleep and the whole house is in utter repose. Dawn reveals towers, and counting each of the leaves one by one, it decks me out in a suit of crinkling lace.

I am forgetting something … I haven't the slightest doubt … it's taken me so long to get ready! …And … Lord, what am I forgetting? Ah, yes. A chunk of wood … a good compact one made of cherry.

I have to be well-groomed when I go … I take a big pale rose, with a furious and hieratic face, from a vase of flowers on the nightstand and tack it to the left lapel of my jacket.

It's time.

(On the bells' uneven salvers come the cocks' crows.)

PÓRTICO

NIÑO: Yo voy por las plumas del pájaro Grifón.
ENANO: Hijo mío, me es imposible ayudarte en esta
          empresa.

                        Cuento popular

    Tan-tan

El aire se había muerto.
Estaba inmóvil y arrugado.

Los pinos yacían en tierra.
Sus sombras de pie, ¡temblando!

    Yo-Tú-Él
    (en un solo plano)

    Tan-tan

[…]

PORTICO

CHILD: I'm going after the feathers of the Griffin-Bird.
DWARF: Child, I cannot be of help in this undertaking.

Folk tale

    Knock-knock

The breeze had died.
Motionless and wrinkled.

The pine-trees lay on the earth.
Their shadows stood, trembling!

    Me-You-Him
    (in one shot)

    Knock-knock

[…]

PERSPECTIVA

Dentro de mis ojos
se abre el canto hermético
de las simientes que
no florecieron.

Todas sueñan un fin
irreal y distinto.
(El trigo sueña enormes
flores amarillentas.)

Todas sueñan extrañas
aventuras de sombra.
Frutos inaccesibles
y vientos amaestrados.

Ninguna se conoce.
Ciegas y descarriadas,
les duelen sus perfumes
enclaustrados por siempre.

Cada semilla piensa
un árbol genealógico
que cubre todo el cielo
de tallos y racimos.

Por el aire se extienden
vegetaciones increíbles.
Ramas negras y grandes,
rosas color ceniza.

PERSPECTIVE

Inside my eyes the
hermetic song opens
of seeds that did not
flower.

They all dream
distant, unreal ends.
(The wheat dreams
enormous yellow flowers.)

They all dream strange
shadow adventures.
Of fruit inaccessible
and domesticated winds.

None is as we know them.
Blind and misguided,
they feel the pain
of forever cloistered scent.

Each seed dreams
of a family tree
that will cover the sky
with its shoots and branches.

Incredible vegetation
grows in the air.
Boughs black and great,
roses the colour of ash.

La luna, casi ahogada
de flores y ramajes,
se defiende con sus rayos
como un pulpo de plata.

Dentro de mis ojos
se abre el canto hermético
de las simientes que
no florecieron.

The moon, almost choked
with flowers and branches,
holds its rays up in protest
like an octopus of silver.

Inside my eyes the
hermetic song opens
of seeds that did not flower.

EL JARDÍN

Jamás nació, ¡jamás!
Pero pudo brotar.

Cada segundo se
profundiza y renueva.

Cada segundo abre
nuevas sendas distintas.

¡Por aquí! ¡Por allí!
Va mi cuerpo multiplicado.

Atravesando pueblos
o dormido en el mar.

¡Todo está abierto! Existen
llaves para las claves.
Pero el sol y la luna
nos pierden y despistan,
y bajo nuestros pies
se enmarañan los caminos.

Aquí contemplo todo
lo que pude haber sido.
Dios o mendigo,
agua o vieja margarita.

Mis múltiples senderos
teñidos levemente
hacen una gran rosa
alrededor de mi cuerpo.

THE GARDEN

Never born, never!
But it could spring into life.

Every second it is
deeper and replenished.

Every second opens
new and different paths.

Over here! Over there!
My body multiplies before my eyes.

Crossing countryside
or lulled upon the sea.

Everything is open! There are
keys for every code.
But the sun and the moon
throw us off track,
and under our feet
the roads grow entangled.

From here I see all
I could once have been.
A beggar or a god,
water or old daisy.

My multifarious paths,
tinged with red,
form one great rose
around me.

Como un mapa imposible,
el jardín de lo posible.
Cada segundo se
profundiza y renueva.

Jamás nació, ¡jamás!
¡Pero pudo brotar!

GLORIETA

Sobre el surtidor inmóvil
duerme un gran pájaro muerto.

Los dos amantes se besan
entre fríos cristales de sueño.

'La sortija, ¡dame la sortija!'
'No sé dónde están mis dedos.'
'¿No me abrazas?' 'Me dejé los brazos
cruzados y fríos en el lecho.'

Entre las hojas se arrastraba
un rayo de luna viejo.

Like an impossible map,
my garden of possibility.
Every second it
grows deeper, is replenished.

Never born, never!
But it could spring into life!

ARBOUR

A great dead bird
asleep on the motionless fountain.

Two lovers kiss
between cold, glass dreams.

'The ring, give me the ring!'
'I don't know where my fingers are!'
'Won't you hold me?' 'I left my arms
folded up in bed, gone cold.'

A ray of waning moon.
crept among the leaves.

AVENIDA

Las blancas Teorías
con los ojos vendados
danzaban por el bosque.

Lentas como cisnes
y amargas como adelfas.

Pasaron sin ser vistas
por los ojos del hombre,
como de noche pasan
inéditos los ríos,
como por el silencio
un rumor nuevo y único.

Alguna entre su túnica
lleva una gris mirada
pero de moribundo.
                    Otras
agitan largos ramos
de palabras confusas.
No viven y están vivas.
Van por el bosque extático.
¡Enjambre de sonámbulas!
(Lentas como cisnes
y amargas como adelfas.)

AVENUE

White-clad Theories
with blindfolded eyes
went dancing through the woods.

As slow as swans,
as bitter as oleander.

They went by undetected
in the eyes of man,
the way rivers go by
unheard of in the night,
the way new and singular sound
moves in the silence.

Some of them bear
a grey but dying look
amid their tunics.
                              Others
wave long branches
of indistinct words.
They are not alive and yet they live.
Moving through ecstatic woods.
A swarm of sleepwalkers!
(Slow as swans,
bitter as oleander).

PARÉNTESIS

Las doncellas dejan un olor
mental ausente de miradas.
El aire se queda indiferente,
camelia blanca de cien hojas.

CANCIÓN DEL JARDINERO INMÓVIL

Lo que no sospechaste
vive y tiembla en el aire.

Al tesoro del día
apenas si tocáis.

Van y vienen cargados
sin que los mire nadie.

Vienen rotos pero vírgenes
y hechos semilla salen.

Os hablan las cosas y
vosotros no escucháis.

El mundo es un surtidor
fresco, distinto y constante.

Al tesoro del día
apenas si tocáis.

PARENTHESIS

The maidens shed an absent
mental scent of someone
never looked at. The air is left cold.
White camellia of a hundred petals.

SONG OF THE MOTIONLESS GARDENER

What you never dreamt of
is alive and trembling in the air.

The treasure each day brings you
lies almost untouched.

Days come and go laden with riches
and no one sees them.

They come in pieces though virgin
still. And they go forth as seed.

Things talk to you,
and you do not listen.

The world is a fountain,
fresh and constantly differing.

The treasure each day brings you
lies almost untouched.

Os veda el puro silencio
el torrente de la sangre.

Pero dos ojos tenéis
para remontar los cauces.

Al tesoro del día
apenas si tocáis.

Lo que no sospechaste
vive y tiembla en el aire.

El jardín se enlazaba
por sus perfumes estancados.

Cada hoja soñaba
un sueño diferente.

The torrent of blood
blocks your way to silence.

But you have eyes to see
to go back upstream.

The treasure each day brings you
lies almost untouched.

What you never dreamt of
is alive and trembling in the air.

Back and forth the garden wove
its pent-up perfume.

Every leaf was dreaming
a different dream.

LOS PUENTES COLGANTES

¡Oh qué gran muchedumbre,
invisible y renovada,
la que viene a este jardín
a descansar para siempre!

Cada paso en la Tierra
nos lleva a un mundo nuevo.
Cada pie lo apoyamos
sobre un puente colgante.

Comprendo que no existe
el camino derecho.
Sólo un gran laberinto
de encrucijadas múltiples.

Constantemente crean
nuestros pies al andar
inmensos abanicos
de senderos en germen.

¡Oh jardín de las blancas
teorías! ¡Oh jardín
de lo que no soy pero
pude y debí haber sido!

THE HANGING BRIDGES

Oh what a great and invisible,
endlessly milling crowd,
the one that comes to this garden
for eternal repose!

Every step on Earth
leads us to a different world.
Every time we set foot
it is on a hanging bridge.

I understand there's no such thing
as the straight path through.
There is only one great labyrinth
of multiplying crossroads.

Enormous fans
display at our feet
as we walk,
pathways in germ.

Oh garden of white
theories! Oh garden of
what I am not
but could and should have been!

EL SÁTIRO BLANCO

Sobre narcisos inmortales
dormía el sátiro blanco.

Enormes cuernos de cristal
virginizaban su ancha frente.

El sol como un dragón vencido
lamía sus largas manos de doncella.

Flotando sobre el rio del amor
todas las ninfas muertas desfilaban.

El corazón del sátiro en el viento
se oreaba de viejas tempestades.

La siringa en el suelo era una fuente
con siete azules caños cristalinos.

THE WHITE SATYR

On a bed of unfading jonquils
the white satyr slept.

Enormous horns of glass
virginified his brow.

The sun like a beaten dragon
licked his long maiden hands.

On the river of love, floating, went
all the dead nymphs in procession.

Gusts of old tempests
blew through the satyr's heart.

On the ground the panpipe was a fountain
of seven blue glass reeds.

ESTAMPAS DEL JARDÍN

[I]

Las antiguas doncellas
que no fueron amadas
vienen con sus galanes
entre las quietas ramas.

Los galanes sin ojos
y ellas sin palabras
se adornan con sonrisas
como plumas rizadas.

Desfilan bajo grises
tulipanes de escarcha
en un blanco delirio
de luces enclaustradas.

La ciega muchedumbre
de los perfumes vaga
con los pies apoyados
sobre flores intactas.

¡Oh luz honda y oblicua
de las yertas naranjas!
Los galanes tropiezan
con sus rotas espadas.

GARDEN PICTURES

[I]

Yesterday's young
unloved maidens
stroll with their suitors
through the unmoving trees.

The young suitors, without eyes
and they, without words,
decked out in smiles
like long, furling plumes.

They promenade
beneath grey tulips of frost
in a white delirium
of cloistered lights.

Feet treading
intact flowers,
the blind throng
of perfumes meanders.

Oh deep, oblique light
of frozen oranges!
The suitors stumble
on their broken swords.

[II]

La viuda de la luna
¿quién la olvidará?
Soñaba que la tierra
fuese de cristal.

Enfurecida y pálida,
quería dormir al mar,
peinando sus melenas
con gritos de coral.

Sus cabellos de vidrio
¿quién los olvidará?
En su pecho los cien
labios de un manantial.

Alabardas de largos
surtidores la van
guardando por las ondas
quietas del arenal.

Pero la luna luna
¿cuándo volverá?
La cortina del viento
tiembla sin cesar.

La viuda de la luna
¿quién la olvidará?
Soñaba que la tierra
fuese de cristal.

II

The widowed moon,
who can forget her?
She dreamt the world
was made of glass.

Furious and pale,
she wanted to rock the sea to sleep,
combing out its tresses
with hard cries of coral.

Her crystal tresses,
who can forget them?
Falling on her breast
like the hundred lips of a spring.

Halberds of long
fountain spray
are guarding her
by the sand's still waves.

But the moon – the real moon-
when it will come back?
The curtain of the wind
is ever atremble.

The widowed moon,
who can forget her?
She dreamt the earth
was made of glass.

Como el buen conde Arnaldo
¿quién te olvidará?
También soñaba toda
la tierra de cristal.

[YO]

[…]

Yo
¿Qué quieres de mí
que no me dejas, Sueño?

Sueño
Doce cisnes de oro
y doce lunas negras.

Yo
Quiero días y noches
claros y sin secretos.

Sueño
[…]

Like the good Count Arnaldo,
who can forget you?
He also dreamt the entire
earth was of glass.

[ME]

[…]

Me:
What do you want of me
that you will not let me be, Dreamworld?

Dreamworld
Twelve golden swans and
twelve black moons.

Me:
I want days and nights
that are bright and have no secrets.

Dreamworld
[…]

ARCO DE LUNAS

Un arco de lunas negras
sobre el mar sin movimiento.

Mis hijos que no han nacido
me persiguen.

'¡Padre, no corras, espera!
El más chico viene muerto.'
Se cuelgan de mis pupilas.
Canta el gallo.

El mar hecho piedra ríe
su última risa de olas.
'¡Padre, no corras!'
                    Mis gritos
se hacen nardos.

MOONBOW

A bow of black moons
in an arc on the unruffled sea.

My unborn children
pursue me.

'Father, wait, don't run!
The youngest one is dead.'
They hang from my eyes.
The cock crows.

The stony-faced sea lets out
its last laughing wave.
'Father, don't run!
                    My cries
are spikenard.

[ALTAS TORRES]

Altas torres.
Largos ríos.

Hada
Toma el anillo de bodas
de tus abuelos.
Cien manos bajo la tierra
lo echarán de menos.

Yo
Voy a sentir en mis manos
una inmensa flor de dedos,
y el símbolo del anillo
¡no lo quiero!

Altas torres.
Largos ríos.

[HIGH TOWERS]

High towers.
Long rivers.

Fairy
Take your grandparents'
wedding ring.
A hundred hands beneath the earth
will ask where it is.

Me
I am going to feel fingers
blossom in my hands,
and the symbol of the ring,
I do not want it!

High towers.
Long rivers.

CANCIONCILLA DEL NIÑO
QUE NO NACIÓ

¡Me habéis dejado sobre una flor
de oscuros sollozos de agua!

El llanto que aprendí
se pondrá viejecito
arrastrando su cola
de suspiros y lágrimas.

Sin brazos, ¿cómo empujo
la puerta de la Luz?
Sirvieron a otro niño
de remos en su barca.

Yo dormía tranquilo.
¿Quién taladró mi sueño?
Mi madre tiene ya
la cabellera blanca.

¡Me habéis dejado sobre una flor
de oscuros sollozos de agua.

LITTLE DITTY OF THE CHILD
THAT WAS NOT BORN

You left me sitting on a blossom
of dark, sobbing waters!

The crying I learned
will grow old and feeble,
dragging its train
of sighs and tears.

Without arms how am I to push
at the doorway to Light?
My arms were another child's
oars for his boat.

I was sleeping peacefully.
Who bore into my dream?
My mother's hair already
is like snow.

You left me sitting on a blossom
of dark, sobbing waters!

CANCIÓN DEL MUCHACHO
DE SIETE CORAZONES

Siete corazones
tengo.
Pero el mío no lo encuentro.

En el alto monte, madre,
tropezábamos yo y el viento.
Siete niñas de largas manos
me llevaron en sus espejos.

He cantado por el mundo
con mi boca de siete pétalos.
Mis galeras de amaranto
iban sin jarcias y sin remos.

He vivido los paisajes
de otras gentes. Mis secretos
alrededor de la garganta
¡sin darme cuenta! iban abiertos.

En el alto monte, madre,
(mi corazón sobre los ecos
dentro del álbum de una estrella)
tropezábamos yo y el viento.

Siete corazones
tengo.
Pero el mío no lo encuentro.

SONG OF THE SEVEN-HEARTED BOY

Seven hearts
have I.
But my own I cannot find.

High in the hills, mother, the wind and I
bumped into one another.
Seven girls with lovely long hands
bore me away in their looking-glasses.

I have sung the world over
with my mouth of seven petals.
My galleys of amaranth
had neither rigging nor oars.

I have known and lived
other peoples' worlds. The secrets
around my throat were open
and I was unaware.

High in the hills, mother
(my heart on the echo in
the album of a star), the wind and I
bumped into one another.

Seven hearts
have I.
But my own I cannot find.

OLOR BLANCO

¡Oh qué frío perfume
de jacintos!

Por los cipreses blancos
viene una doncella.
Trae los senos cortados
en un plato de oro.

(Dos caminos.
Su larguísima cola
y la Vía Láctea.)

Madre
de los niños muertos,
tiembla con el delirio
de los gusanos de luz.

¡Oh qué frío perfume
de jacintos!

WHITE SCENT

Oh what a cold perfume
of hyacinths!

A maiden comes walking
through the white cypresses.
She bears a golden platter
with her severed white breasts.

(Two paths.
Her impossibly long train
and the Milky Way.)

The mother of
dead children
trembles with a glowworm
delirium.

Oh what a cold perfume
of hyacinths!

ENCUENTRO

Flor de sol.
Flor de río.

Yo
¿Eras tú? Tienes el pecho
iluminado y no te he visto.

Ella
¡Cuántas veces te han rozado
las cintas de mi vestido!

Yo
Sin abrir, oigo en tu garganta
las blancas voces de mis hijos.

Ella
Tus hijos flotan en mis ojos
como diamantes amarillos.

Yo
¿Eras tú? ¿Por dónde arrastrabas
esas trenzas sin fin, amor mío?

Ella
En la luna. ¿Te ríes? Entonces,
alrededor de la flor del narciso.

Yo
En mi pecho se agita sonámbula
una sierpe de besos antiguos.

ENCOUNTER

Sun flower.
River flower.

Me
Was that you? Your breast
is glowing and I did not see you.

Her
How many times the ribbons on my dress
brushed past you!

Me
In your unopened throat I hear
my children's white voices.

Her
Your children float in my eyes
like yellow diamonds.

Me
Was it you? Where were you trailing
those endless tresses, my love?

Her
On the moon. Are you laughing? Then
around the flower of the narcissus.

Me
In my breast a serpent of old kisses
stirs in its sleep.

Ella
Los instantes abiertos clavaban
sus raíces sobre mis suspiros.

Yo
Enlazados por la misma brisa
frente a frente ¡no nos conocimos!

Ella
El ramaje se espesa, vete pronto.
¡Ninguno de los dos hemos nacido!

Flor de sol.
Flor de río.

Her
The opened instants
sank roots into my sighs.

Me
Joined by the same breeze,
face to face, we were strangers!

Her
Go now, the branches thicken around us.
Neither one of us has been born!

Sun flower.
River flower.

DUNA

Sobre la extensa duna
de la luz antiquísima
me encuentro despistado
sin cielo ni camino.

El Norte moribundo
apagó sus estrellas.
Los cielos naufragados
se ondulaban sin prisa.

Por el mar de la luz
¿dónde voy? ¿A quién busco?
Aquí gime el reflejo
de las lunas veladas.

¡Ay, mi fresco pedazo
de madera compacta,
vuélveme a mi balcón
y a mis pájaros vivos!

El jardín seguirá
moviendo sus arriates
sobre la ruda espalda
del silencio encallado.

DUNES

On the vast dunes
of ancient light
I am utterly confounded,
without path or sky.

The dying North
switched off all its stars.
Shipwrecked skies
undulated, slowly,

Through the sea of light
where do I go? Whom do I seek?
The reflection
of veiled moons is moaning.

If only my lucky piece
of fine-grained wood,
could take me back
to my balcony and my living birds!

The garden will keep on
shifting its borders
over the rough shoulder
of silence run aground.

¡AMANECER Y REPIQUE!

Fuera del jardín

El sol con sus cien cuernos
levanta el cielo bajo.

El mismo gesto repiten
los toros en la llanura.

La pedrea estremecida
de los viejos campanarios

despierta y pone en camino
al gran rebaño del viento.

En el río ahora comienzan
las batallas de los peces.

¡Alma mía, niño y niña,
¡¡silencio!!

DAWN AND PEALING BELLS

Outside the garden

A sun of one hundred horns
lifts the hooded sky.

On the prairie the bulls
also lift their heads.

The old belltowers
fling their stones

to waken the wind herd
and drive it down the road.

In the river now the fish
commence their battles.

My soul, boy and girl,
be silent, silent!

APPENDIX

[YO]

YO

¡Ah fantasma esquelético,
árbol lleno de nieve,
chopo de todas
las pasiones!

No hay hacha que logre
talar tu madera
ni llama que abarque
tus brazos enhiestos.
Continuas siempre.
Eres magnífico.
Eterno.

YO

¡Guardián de la humanidad!
Espanta-querubes
y espanta-virtudes.
Debieras llevar sable
y casco.

YO

Imperativo.
Nido
del águila del *Más*.

[I]

I

Oh you skeletal wraith!
Tree full of snow.
Poplar
of all passions

There isn't an axe can
fell your timber
nor flame that can envelop
your upright arms.
You go on forever.
You are magnificent.
Eternal.

I

The guardian of humanity!
Scourge of cherubs.
Scourge of virtues.
You ought to wear
a saber and a helmet.

I

Imperious.
Aerie
of More.

YO

Me siento atravesado
por la grave Y griega
(bieldo de académicos,
toro del alfabeto)
y la O cual corona
de tinta a mis pies.

I

I feel I've been run through
by the great grave Y
(winnowing-fork of academics,
bull of the alphabet)
and the M like a crown
of ink at my feet.

DIURNO

A Guillermo de Torre

I

CIUDAD

La torre dice: 'Hasta aquí'
y el ciprés: 'Yo más allá.'

Hombres y mujeres hacen
la Babel de las palabras.

Avanzan por los tejados
violentos zigzag y elipses.

La ciudad adorna su frente
con plumas de humo y silbidos.

Todos buscan lo que no
podrán encontrar jamás

y la hierba crece ante
el pórtico del Allí.

DIURNAL DIPTYCH

For Guillermo de Torre

I

CITY

The tower says: 'Up to here'.
and the cypress tree: 'Beyond.'

Men and women make
the Tower of Babel of words.

Angry zigzags and ellipses
advance along the rooftops.

The city's brow is decked
with whistles and plumes of smoke.

They are all looking for what
they will never be able to find

And grass grows in front of
the gateway to the beyond.

II

REACCIÓN

¡Corazón mío, vete
con las sabias tortugas,
corazón mío, por
un Sahara de luz!

De pontifical
con sus capas pluviales,
las tortugas enseñan
lo inútil de los pies.

Saben las falsedades
de horizontes celestes,
y dedican su vida
a estudiar una estrella
con la que
impregnan el carey.

Corazón mío, vete
con las sabias tortugas.
Hélice para el cuerpo
y alas para el espíritu
no te harán falta cuando
sientas andar la Tierra.

Corazón mío, apaga
tu vieja sed de límites.

II

REACTION

Go off with the sage tortoises,
heart.
Over a Sahara of light,
heart.

Pontifical
in their copes,
the tortoises show us
how useless feet are.

They know the untruths
of celestial horizons
and so devote their lives
to the study of one star
permeating their shell.

Go off with the tortoises,
heart.
You'll have no need
of a propeller for your body
or wings for your spirit
once you feel the earth move beneath you.

Quench your old thirst
for limits, heart.

NOCHE

Estrellas amaestradas.
Circo azul.
Doña Luna sonríe
(Salomé centenaria).
Venus tiene un penacho
de plumas.

Arena de niebla.
Lámparas de sueños.
Caballitos luceros
van y vienen
salpicando rocío
y luz de amanecer.

¡Oh corazón mío,
corazón sin alas,
da tu salto mortal
sobre el arco de la noche!

NIGHT

Stars that have learnt their tricks.
A blue circus.
Lady Moon smiles
(centennial Salomé).
Venus sports a crest
of fine feathers.

An arena of mist.
Lamps from out of a dream.
Little pony stars
trip back and forth
splashing dew
and light from the break of day.

Oh heart of mine,
heart with wings,
somersault over
the archway of the night!

[EL CAMPO SEGADO]

El campo segado
y la luna disuelta.

Por el aire van los sueños
de las semillas.
Espiga azul
y amapola blanca.

Mi alma,
una sola flor
delirante.

El campo segado
y la luna disuelta.

TIERRA

Las niñas de la brisa
van con sus largas colas.

CIELO

Los mancebos del aire
saltan sobre la luna.

[MOWN FIELD]

Mown field,
moonlight dissolving.

Seeds' dreams
go up in the air.
A blue ear of grain,
a white poppy.

My soul,
the only delirious
flower.

Mown field,
moonlight dissolving.

EARTH

Girls of the breeze
go by in trailing skirts

SKY

Young men of the air
jump over the moon

[UN NIÑO ACABA DE NACER]

Un niño acaba de nacer.
Me lo ha dicho una estrella.
Y vengo con mis gotas de cristal
y mis cadencias
a darle la primera
lección poética,
a enseñarle el encanto
de las verdes praderas
perdidas en el fondo
de las sierras.
Corono con mis flores de sonido
su cabeza
y mi lengua de cobre
borra sus penas.
El niño es mi oveja.
Pero estoy muy lejos de su sueño.
Yo canto entre la niebla.
Preocupado en mi propia
tristeza.
Turbia melancolía
de plata vieja.

[A CHILD HAS JUST BEEN BORN]

A child has just been born.
A star told me.
And I come with my cadences
and crystal drops
to give him his first
lesson in poetry,
to teach him the charm
of green meadows
lost at the back
of the mountains.
I crown his head
with flowers of sound
and my copper tongue
rubs away his woes.
The child
is my sheep.
But I am very far from his dream.
I sing in the fog.
Immersed in my own
sadness.
Tarnished melancholy
of old silver.

NOTES

RÍO AZUL / BLUE RIVER: From an undated ms. Christopher Maurer places the composition between late 1920 and early 1922 (*CP* 906). García-Posada considers this an incomplete *suite* (*OC* I, 696–99); the first poem was blocked off in the ms, as if to reject it; I have restored it in order to make the poem viable, as does Maurer.

The title and the idea of the ivory ship that can bear away the old (kisses, poems) might be inspired in Rubén Darío and the lines that headed the little magazine *Grecia*, a journal which moved from *modernismo* to *ultraísmo*. The readers of numbers 1 to 43 of the journal would have seen these lines on the first page of each issue:

'En la angustia de la ignorancia / del porvenir, saludemos / la barca llena de fragancia / que tiene de marfil los remos'.

[In the anguish of our ignorance / of the future, let us salute / the boat full of fragrance / whose oars are made of ivory].

The lines are from Darío's 'Programa matinal', *Cantos de vida y esperanza* (1905).

In a prose poem from 1921 titled 'Telégrafo' Lorca associates the image of a blue river with an 'odd country' (*raro país*) floating above it to which he goes off in a reverie (see *OC* I, 665.)

It is interesting to note that two older writers with whom Lorca came into contact used the image in works published in 1923. Juan Ramón Jimenez speaks of a 'blue river of existence' in a poem titled 'La obra' from *Belleza* (*en verso 1917–1923*) (Madrid: Juan Ramón Jimenez y Zenobia Camprubí de Jiménez, 1923):

por la orilla segunda / del río azul de la existencia / viendo el pasado, la primera orilla,/ reflejando en el agua de la tarde / su májica hermosura universal (p. 118)

[along the second shore of the blue river of existence / watching the past, the first shore, / reflecting its magic, universal beauty / on the water of the evening].

Yet Ramón Gómez de la Serna (*El alba y otras cosas*, Madrid: Editorial 'Saturnino Calleja', 1923) comes closest to Lorca's meaning:

> Hay un río azul, turbio de azulosidad, que es el que se lleva todas las juventudes, el río en que se desahogan todos los romanticismos, el río al que echan los poetas sus poemas partidos en pedacitos o dobladillados en forma de barco. (p. 146)

> [There is a blue river, dark with the essence of blue, which is the one that carries off everyone's youth, the river in which all varieties of romanticism unburden themselves, the river where poets throw their poems torn into pieces or folded into the shape of a boat.]

In the first untitled poem in the *suite*: *Besos*, line 4 ('kisses') may be a metaphor for his poems, as Lorca suggests in a letter to the young guitarist Regino Sainz de la Maza, dated December 1920: 'My hands are full of dead kisses (apples of snow with the tremulous furrow of lips) and I hope to toss them into the broken air in order to find new ones' (*E* 94).
'Dreams': Notice the nod in the direction of the avant-garde in the metaphor ('the moon's bald pate') with its irreverent treatment of the moon, a *bête noire* for the anti-Romantic Futurists.

NOCHE / NIGHT: Maurer (*CP* 901) suggests this poem is from July 1921. It may, however, be the poem which Lorca refers to as a *suite*, in a letter to his family written on 29 March 1921 (*E* 105). There he describes a poem which he would like friends Adolfo Salazar and Robert Gerhard to set to music. What is unusual here are the allusions to sound; the poem is not, strictly speaking, oriented around visual images, as we will find in most of the *suites.*
'Swath': A *pájaro pinto* is a bright red bird found in old folksong about love as in the lines, 'Bien te estavas en tu nido, / páxaro pinto' [And you were so cosy in your nest / little red bird], No. 518 in Margit Frenk, *Corpus antiguo de la lírica popular hispánica* (Madrid: Castalia, 1987). In a children's song dating back to the seventeenth-century the female bird is featured, the *pájara pinta*. The song accompanies a circle game in which a child chooses a girl or boyfriend.
'Mother': The 'Great Mother Bear' is the constellation Ursus Major.
'Kite': The word *cometa* in the original's title can mean either 'comet' or 'kite'. The child's toy suggests that there may be children on Sirius,

the star that is associated with the dog days, the hottest time of summer. The *suite* appeared in *Indice*, No. 4 (1922).

SUITE DE LOS ESPEJOS / MIRROR SUITE: This *suite* is dated 15 April 1921. The mirror imagery interlocks with the fantasy of the last *suite* and the world behind the looking-glass. Significantly, there is an emphasis here on the secrets held therein and the location of a garden where true love awaits. See also 'Sesame' (*Moments of Song*).
'Reflection': A poem that plays with the perception of what is near and far. A moth seen up close can blot out the image of the full moon in the sky.
'Capriccio', lines 7–8: 'a nest of silences / that have not taken wing': a hint that behind the looking-glass are secrets that could be released
'The Eyes': The poet envisages a lady gardener (Death); but in the 'Song of the Motionless Gardener' (*In the Garden of the Lunar Grapefruits)* the figure is masculine and seems to have the powers of both life and death.

In the same poem, the 'Castle of No Return' (*el castillo de irás y no volverás*) refers to a place in traditional folktales. The little girl Elena embroiders cravats (*corbatas*) like the heroine of a children's ballad who was stolen away by an ungrateful guest.

This *suite* was published in Juan Ramón Jiménez's little magazine *Indice*, No. 3 (1921).

EL JARDÍN DE LAS MORENAS / THE GARDEN OF THE DARK-HAIRED GIRLS: One of Lorca's first publications in a new mode, it appeared in *Indice*, No. 2 (1921), the little magazine published by Juan Ramón Jiménez. Maurer (*CP* 901) dates it tentatively to July 1921.
'Acacia' figures also in the *Water Suite*.
'Lemongrove': In the final line, note the absence of either the phallic symbol (the walking-stick) or the symbol of a girl's virginity (the rose).

In traditional Iberian love lyric the lemon is contrasted with the orange to suggest unrequited or unconsummated love as opposed to a love that is mutually felt and fulfilled, with the promise of offspring.

CAPRICHOS / CAPRICCIOS: Dated 9 July 1921. This *suite* shows some of the playful spirit of Ramón Gómez de la Serna, who was influential in Madrid's early avant-garde. In some of his *greguerías* (humorous conceits) he played with the significance of the different letters of the alphabet. In the original, one can read an acrostic in the highlighted letters: *l-u-m*, the root of words derived from the Latin having to do with light.

MOMENTOS DE CANCIÓN / MOMENTS OF SONG: A *suite* dated 10 July 1921. It is possibly one that Lorca referred to in a letter to Adolfo Salazar (2 August 1921): 'I call these things "songs with a reflection", because that is what I want to do: give the sublime sensation of a reflection with words, taking away from their trembling all that makes it spiral and curve' ('quitando … todo lo que tiene de salomónico') (*E* 123–24).
'Song with a Reflection': The cypress tree is traditionally associated with death, as it is often planted in cemeteries. This poem, like 'Eco' (from *Canciones*, *OC* I, 401), plays with the idea of a memory as an echo lost in the past.
'Sesame': As in 'open, sesame'. In his parable of the cave in *The Republic*, Plato holds that we mistake a reflection of eternal shapes for the real. Lorca appears to emphasize the reigning specularity.

Hermes Trimegistis, the mythical founder of hermetic thought, taught that 'as above, so below', or, as in the heavens, so on earth – the universe is envisioned as a myriad system of reflections.

The hermetic view sees mirroring everywhere, between what lies above and what is on earth, what is inside ourselves and what is without. It may be that the idea there is 'one heart and only one wind' is an excess in Lorca's early poetry, an idea that seeps into the *suites* from the margins, from an unidentified hermetic text. In context, the image speaks of the seat of emotion and the winds of time, and so, intuitively, of the continuity of our desire as we move through life.

But also in context: the speaker is offering counsel to the heart. 'You cannot reach the object of your desire, no matter whether you are near it or far. It is as if you were seeking it in a mirror.' And there only remains to say, 'Seek inside the mirror'.

Line 9: *[E]l gran vuelo* is literally 'the great flight' when the soul returns whence it came. What will happen to love at the end of time?
'Tearful Song': The ms shows that Lorca had hesitations about publishing this particular poem, as he bracketed it in its entirety. Perhaps it seemed too overtly sentimental. I translate *lirio* as 'iris', bearing in mind an early article by Ian Gibson ('Lorca's "Balada triste"', see

Bibliography) in which he argues that this flower is what a very young Lorca contrasted with the conventional rose that he 'lost' in childhood.
The Song Sets': Dedicated to the young musicologist Adolfo Salazar. Leslie Stainton notes the poet's performance of a poem that is surely this one: 'To suggest the moon opening and closing its 'tail', Lorca 'moved his thick hands back and forth like a fan' (Lorca, *A Dream of Life*, New York, Farrar Straus and Giroux, 1990, p. 119).

PALIMPSESTOS / PALIMPSESTS: This *suite* is undated but may go back to the summer of 1921. It is one of four included in *Primeras canciones* (1936), published by Manuel Altolaguirre and Concha Méndez as a small anthology of unpublished verse. This is the edition followed here, as in the *OC*. Maurer gives a version from 1926 or 1927, including two more poems titled 'Aire' and 'Madrigal' (see *CP*, 214–16), which to my mind make the *suite* more heterogeneous.

Lorca's title refers to a parchment in which the original writing was effaced in order for another text to be written on it. Yet a palimpsest, as Lorca would have it, is a complex metaphor for the action of time, and for the act of writing these poems, in which a sentiment or memory or even a desire disappears as the text progresses, accentuating a performative quality in the texts. See Quance, *In the Light*, 111–16.

Painter and poet José Moreno Villa was a mentor for the students at Madrid's *Residencia de Estudiantes*. He appears to have inspired Lorca's early interest, around 1924, in the *rosa mutabilis*, an image central to *Doña Rosita the Spinster* (1935).
'Gallery': Night engulfs the men who have taken up different positions vis-à-vis desire. Lorca relies on the reader's knowing that in the traditional ballads a hunter pursues love in contrast with the monks, who abstain.

CANCIONES BAJO LA LUNA / SONGS BENEATH THE MOON: Christopher Maurer believes the *suite* may be incomplete (with a final page or pages missing), and dates it to July 1921, 'probably' (*CP* 904). On the theme of Salomé, it is interesting to note that in *Indice*, No. 1 (1921), Juan Ramón Jiménez's little magazine, the philosopher José Ortega y Gasset had published 'Esquema de Salomé', an essay which suggests that Salomé was more masculine than feminine. A likely influence for both would have been Oscar Wilde.

'*Full Moon*': Under the title 'La luna asoma' and in a different version, this poem heads the section 'Canciones de luna' in *Canciones* (1927). A small but significant variation in lines 3 and 4 in the first stanza appears. In *Canciones* we read 'y aparecen las sendas / impenetrables' [and impenetrable / paths appear]. Instead of the last stanza as given here, Lorca wrote two stanzas that move away from the emphasis on faded memory: 'Nobody eats oranges / under the full moon. / One must eat / green and icy fruit. // When the full moon of a hundred / identical faces is up, / silver coins / sob in your pocket.'

'*Salomé and the Moon*', line 15: Traditionally a man's good looks were summed up in the refrain: 'El hombre y el oso, cuanto más feo, más hermoso' [Man and bear, the homelier, the better-looking].

ESTAMPAS DEL MAR / SEASIDE PICTURES: Undated ms. Here and in the following *suite*, I choose the word *picture* as the way to translate *estampa*, which is not being used in a literal sense (engraving) but as a scene presented to the eye. The poem is dedicated to two poets from Malaga, Manuel Altolaguirre and Emilio Prados, who would bring out the journal *Litoral* in 1927 and who had intended to bring out an edition of *suites* around the same time as *Canciones* (1927). Probably written in July 1921, it was revised in 1926, with two poems removed (Maurer, *CP*, 903).

[*The sea / wants / to lift its lid*]: Lorca captures the dualistic image we have inherited of the mermaid (or siren: both translations are possible). On the one hand they sing and their song is bewitching; on the other hand, they are a peril to sailors. Both senses inform Ulysses' encounter with the sirens in the *Odyssey*.

'*Two Stars of the Sea*': Two archetypal women exchange knowledge about seduction and the homely skill of knitting. Venus is the morning (or evening) star; the Virgin Mary is known as the *stella maris* or 'star of the sea', who guides sailors home.

TRES ESTAMPAS DEL CIELO / THREE PICTURES OF THE HEAVENS: Probably dating from July 1921 (Maurer, *CP* 903), revised in 1923 and again in 1926.

[*The stars*]: First published in *Verso y prosa* [Murcia] in August 1927. Line 8, '…every night through the bars': an allusion to the way courtship was conducted in country towns in Spain in the early 20th century, with women speaking to their lovers on the street from behind the bars on the windows.

'Suitor': '…so he can see his body': Narcissus is a theme that runs throughout the *suites* and Lorca's first book, *Canciones*. Peering into the natural mirror of water, Narcissus needs to see another boy in order to perceive how he looks, or even to confirm that he has a body.

Venus is the subject of Velázquez's painting *The Toilet of Venus* or Titian's painting *Venus Delighting Herself with Love and Music*

FERIAS / FAIRS: This *suite*, dated 27 July 1921, was originally given to the Belgian Hispanist Mathilde Pomès in 1931. It was first published in 1997. I have drawn the text from Maurer's bilingual edition of Lorca's poetry, *CP* 232–46, omitting a stanza (after line 11) from 'Canción morena', which Lorca drew a box around in the ms: 'Me perdería / por tus senos temblantes. / por las hondas negruras / de tu cuerpo suave' [I could get lost / in your trembling breasts, / in the deep darknesses / of your soft body].

The second poem, *'Little Wooden Horses'*, refers to one of the most familiar rides on the merry-go-round and recalls a poem by Antonio Machado: 'Pegasos, lindos pegasos, / caballitos de madera.', in *Poesía y prosa*, vol. 2, 488 .

'Variation': Mambrú is the hero of a popular children's song that came to Spain from France in the eighteenth century. Mambrú went to war and did not return. Three little birds sing on his glass-lidded coffin.

SOMBRA / SHADOW: Ms dated 29 July 1921. There is a fatalistic idealism in the notion that singing (through his poetry) the poet will see 'the only star / that doesn't exist'. The lines of 'Ending' suggest the desolation that the poet will see in the sky in *Poet in New York* ('Canyons of lime imprisoned an empty sky…' 'Dance of Death')

'Village': As Maurer has noted (*CP* 904), the tower is a St Lucy in stone, for, like the saint of legend who had gouged-out eyes, its two towers are empty.

'Ursa Major': The constellation known in Spanish as 'el carro' (the chariot).

An ancient world view, perhaps the one described in Plato's dialogue about the soul, *Phaedrus*, no longer applies. In that dialogue the soul is famously compared to a chariot whose driver strives to control the horses (one of which is good and the beautiful, the other 'entirely the opposite') in an effort to ascend to the heavens (246a–b).

'*Summit*': See the Introduction for comment on this early use of the image of St Sebastian.

CUATRO BALADAS AMARILLAS / FOUR YELLOW BALLADS: This *suite* was probably composed in the summer of 1921 (see *E* 124, where Lorca refers to 'baladas amarillentas' [yellowish ballads]). A final draft from 20 August 1922 exists.

This *suite* was included in *Primeras canciones* (1936) and also published in *Taller* (Mexico), No. 1 (December 1938), from a handwritten copy made by Genaro Estrada in a notebook he took with him to Mexico after the Civil War. The *Suite del agua* and *Herbarios* appeared in the same number of *Taller*, the first in a longer version, since reconstructed. See *OC* I, 899.

In popular verse from the Renaissance, the solitary shepherd is someone who is unlucky in love, as in the lines: 'Aquel pastorcico, madre, / que no viene / algo tiene en el campo/ que le duele' [That little shepherd, mother, / who hasn't come back / has something in the country / making him pine]. This is No. 568A in Margit Frenk, *Corpus de la antigua lírica popular hispánica (siglos XV a XVII)* (Madrid: Castalia, 1987).

II: In the refrain's original Spanish the sense of 'orillo' is hard to translate. Literally, it refers to the coarsely woven edging of a piece of cloth, a selvage (or selvedge). Perhaps the poet is playing with the idea of gold in the signifier, which is what the sounds suggest independently of their dictionary sense. My translation is meant to place the shepherd at the edge of a 'cloth' of (yellow) land.

REMANSOS / POOLS IN THE STREAM: Maurer notes that one ms is dated 12 June 1921, while an autograph ms made in 1927 is dated August 1921 (*CP* 901).

This *suite* was first published with textual and structural variants in *Verso y prosa* [Murcia], 4 (1927) with the subtitle '(Diferencias)' and with an additional poem 'Sigue', in which the poet makes explicit the idea that a *remanso* is a pause in the flow of time: 'Cada lucero, / Un remanso del tiempo. / Un nudo / del tiempo [Every star, a pool / in time. / A knot / in time]. (For the complete text see *OC* I, 850–52).

The text followed here is from *Primeras canciones* (1936), a miscellaneous collection brought out by the poets Manuel Altolaguirre and Concha Méndez and generally held to be an advance of a fuller collection that would have featured *suites*.

Lorca used the term *remanso* metaphorically to refer to a lyrical interlude within a (temporal) stream. In 'Variations' I have taken the liberty of moving in that direction.

HORAS DE VERANO / SUMMER HOURS: From a fair copy dated 10 August 1921

Lorca's *suite* may well have been inspired by a sequence of haiku by José Juan Tablada included in his book *Un día* (Caracas 1919), as Christopher Maurer has observed (*CP* 903).

'[Knifegrinder]': The knifegrinder used to be a familiar figure in cities and villages, as he went through the streets calling out with a distinctive whistle for customers to bring their knives to him to be sharpened on his wheel. Occasionally one may still see a knife-grinder (or knife-sharpener) guiding his bicycle through the city streets in search of customers.

Lines 13–14: A catherine wheel, or breaking wheel, in allusion to the wheel on which St Catherine was tortured, evidence (as in *Shadow*) that Lorca's imagination was fed by the reading of saints' lives.

EL REGRESO / THE RETURN: Lorca's *Epistolario* (125) contains a letter from the author to Adolfo Salazar, 2 August 1921, that contextualizes the sentiment in this *suite*: 'Veo que la vida ya me va echando sus cadenas. La vida tiene razón mucha razón, pero ¡qué lástima de mis alas, ¡qué lástima de mi niñez seca!' [I see that love is putting chains on me. Life has its reasons and good ones, but … what a shame, my withered childhood!] Lorca would claim in 1934 that 'The emotions of my childhood are still in me. I haven't emerged from them' (*OC* III, 523). This ms dates from 6 August 1921 and once consisted of eleven poems. The *suite* was revised in 1923, according to Maurer. In October 1923 Lorca sent the first poem and the text of 'Bend in the River' to his friend Melchor Fernández Almagro.

The revised version appeared in *La Verdad* [Murcia], No. 18, 24 May, 1924 under the title *Suite.*

'The Return' builds on a Platonic theme in the *Phaedrus* (246c) on the doctrine of the soul. The soul originally had wings and will return whence it came if during its long sojourn on earth it is not corrupted. The theme is an important one for Lorca, as evidenced by the fact that it characterizes the predicament of the Young Man in *Once Five Years Pass* (1931).

'Current': *se olvida* (lit., 'forgets himself'). The phrase has a strong connotation of alienation and comes up in a poem from *Canciones*, 'Suicidio', whose protagonist 'se olvidaba'.

'Towards': In the 'clear-flowing springs' there is symbolism derived from a traditional ballad which suggests untroubled love. See 'Fonte-frida' (No. 91) in *Romancero*, ed. Paloma Díaz-Mas (Barcelona: Crítica. 1994).

'Bend in the River': In this poem Lorca uses a variety of *leixa-pren* [lit. set down/pick up] technique, common to medieval Galician-Portuguese lyric. The second line in the first couplet becomes the first in the next, skipping over the refrain, and so on.

The lines about shadow (or shade, 'sombra') echo a traditional lyric which complains about unrequited love: 'Arrimárame a ti, rosa. / No me diste solombra' (I clove to you, rose. / You did not give me shade.) See Margit Frenk, *Corpus de la antigua lírica popular*, no. 651.

The poem is a good example of how Lorca uses the unfolding of the poem to act out a process of diminution and loss. See also 'Galleries' (in *Palimpsests*) and 'Gacela XI. Del amor con cien años' from the *Diván del Tamarit* [Tamarit Oriental Songbook].

Line 3, 'nightingale': From medieval times, the emblem of the lyric poet.

SECRETOS / SECRETS: Ms dated 11 August 1921

'Fountain': 'a still dormant word', an allusion to Lorca's conviction that Christ's gospel is still powerful, an idea that the poet comes back to in *Poet in New York*, when he insists that 'Christ can still give water' ('Grito hacia Roma' [Crying Out to Rome], *OC* I, 562) 'Mirror': In medieval Galician lyric a sash (*cintillo*) was a love token that could be given a young man by his chosen one.

'Mirror': 'lost in the looking-glass': can be linked to the last *suite.*

'Open Door': Doorways often have a symbolic meaning in Lorca as they are the point of contact with the beyond and its mysteries. We see this in the final *suite*, where witches meet the hero at the door of the garden.

Later, in *Poet in New York* the idea of a doorway is extended to the idea of an archway to the beyond and in particular to an empty sky, for Christ's death on the cross is imagined to have been in vain. See 'Abandoned Church': 'I had a son. He got lost amid the arches one Friday of all the dead' (*OC* I, 522).

'Journey': The griffin is a mythical bird with the body, tail, and hind legs of a lion; the head and wings of an eagle; and an eagle's talons as its front feet

Delgadina: The heroine of a well-known traditional ballad, of the same name. She is the object of her father the King's incestuous lust.

ALBUM BLANCO / WHITE ALBUM: Dated 18 August 1921.

In the 19th C. young women often kept albums in which they collected poems and other tributes to their charm offered them by admirers.

The name Eloisa inevitably suggests the story of Abelard and Heloise and their unrequited love.

The poets mentioned in the last poem are Gustavo Alberto Bécquer and José de Espronceda, two Spanish Romantic poets.

'Last Page': Girls were said to have drunk vinegar to whiten their complexion.

In one of his letters to his friend Adolfo Salazar Lorca exclaims of their friendship, 'Love in an album of pretty pictures!' (*E* 140).

The *suite* should be read within the context of the avant-garde's dismissal of sentimentality.

LA SELVA DE LOS RELOJES / THE FOREST OF CLOCKS: This *suite* was first published in Mexico in 1938. 'A Clock's Echo' appeared under the title 'Claro de reloj' [Clearing on the Clock Face] as a freestanding poem in *Primeras canciones*. Maurer dates it hesitantly to August 1921 (*CP* 904) and to the time of *Water Suite*, but imagery in the last poem overlaps with a letter from September 1922. In a letter to his friend, the young guitarist Regino Sainz de la Maza, Lorca claims that he has made a terrible discovery about himself. He has not yet 'been born'. He does not recognize himself. 'The other day I was observing my past intently (I was seated in my grandfather's easy chair) and none of the dead hours belonged to me because I was not the one who had lived them…' There were 'a thousand Federico García Lorcas, lying forever in the attic of time…' (*E* 158).

The image is created of a child lost in the woods where huge grandfather clocks create a deafening din. Pocket watches and clocks pose a challenge insofar as they represent the ticking reminder of tradition. The young poetic subject is wary of finding love as he feels he is expected to do.

'A Clock's Echo': *Claro* might well be translated as a *glade* or a *clearing* in keeping with the forest setting, but I have chosen *pause* to allude to the moment after the clock has struck the hour.

CRUZ / CROSS: A *suite* dated tentatively to autumn 1921 (Maurer, *CP* 906). There are some affinities with the *Poema del cante jondo*, especially with regard to the poem 'South' and the 'arrow of gold'. In 'La guitarra' for example, the instrument weeps like a 'flecha sin blanco' [an arrow without target] in a sign of hopeless desire.

Behind this poem one can detect another nod in the direction of visual poetry, as the four compass points would outline the shape of a cross. Yet there is no sign that the poet would have printed the poem in such a way as to bring this out.

SUITE DEL AGUA / WATER SUITE: Maurer dates this *suite* tentatively to the autumn of 1921. Published in Mexico in 1938, according to a notebook copy made by Lorca's friend Genaro Estrada, it once included the poems now gathered separately into the *suite Cruz* (see Maurer's editorial notes in *CP* 905–906). Neither Maurer nor García-Posada is confident that the last poem 'Beehive' really belongs to this grouping. Note that it picks up a theme (of lovers with glass between them) in 'Arbour' from the last *suite*.

'Curve': As in *Herbals* the opening out onto a cosmic perspective is linked to earthly disappointments.

The poem 'Acacia' is repeated in the 'The Garden of the Dark-Haired Girls'.

TRES CREPÚSCULOS / THREE TWILIGHTS: Written on 1 November 1921 and revised in 1926 (*CP* 906). Maurer observes that this *suite* was written on the same day as the *Poema de la siguiriya gitana*.

III: 'Pierrot's / mandolin', lines 11–12: As Emilio Peral Vega argues, Pierrot or the unhappy clown will become one of the poet's masks, associated with the sadness caused by a repressed sexual identity. See *Pierrot/Lorca. White Carnival of Black Desire* (London: Tamesis, 2015). Pierrot is also, like Pegasus, an allusion to the figure of the *modernista* poet. Both are invoked in the poem 'Parque [Park] (*OC* III, 710–11), which was discarded from the *suites*: 'Among the felled trees / Pegasus lay dead / In each eye he had / an arrow of shadow. // An enormous spider played / the broken mandolin / of that… Oh my God! / Better keep quiet about it!'

PAÍSES / COUNTRIES: Undated ms (only one page found). Christopher Maurer (*CP* 905) conjectures it may be from November 1921.

'Snow', line 7: Technically, a *milano* is a 'kite' or a 'goshawk'. I have settled on 'hawk' in view of the allegorical nature of the image.

HISTORIETAS DEL VIENTO / LITTLE STORIES OF THE WIND: The poem's date is a matter of conjecture: perhaps from July 1922 (Maurer, *CP* 907).

This *suite* was published in a shorter version – with the first three poems – in Murcia in the little magazine *Verso y prosa*, no. 8, August-September (1927). However, in a letter from July 1922 to Melchor Fernández Almagro Lorca described two other poems which had formed part of it: 'Escuela' and 'Rosa'. 'Escuela was published separately in *Verso y prosa*, no. 9 (1927). 'Rosa' was deleted from the ms, but Maurer inserts it before 'Escuela' in his edition. I retain both, as the little poem contributes to the love theme with its playful interpretation of the compass-rose and the punctuation sign.

In his letter to Fernández (*E* 150) Lorca declares he is pleased with the topic of the wind: 'How admirable and how full of different perspectives the wind is!' The last poem is linked to 'Arbolé, arbolé, seco y verdé' (Tree, dried up and green, *Canciones*), which has a more negative valence than is in evidence here. The young girl (who is symbolically the tree) does not take a human lover, preferring instead the wind's embrace.

ENSUEÑOS DEL RÍO / RIVERSIDE REVERIES: This *suite* is from July–August 1922. The unfinished composition is mentioned in a letter to Melchor Fernández Almagro (*E* 155).

The rivers that are named in this suite (the Cubillas and the Genil) are rivers near the town of Fuente Vaqueros, where Lorca was born.

The first poem appears with minor revisions as one of the *Canciones* under the title 'Preludio' (*OC* III, 403–404).

'Lazy Current': Laced with motifs from traditional folksong, which associate the river with love. For example: 'Por el río, me llevad amigo, / y llevádeme por el río' [Down the river, take me, my love / and take me down the river]. The eyes are a synecdoche often used to name the lover or the beloved: the subject who sees or the object who is seen. See Margit Frenk, *Corpus de la antigua lírica popular hispánica (siglos XV a XVII)* (Madrid: Castalia, 1987) for No. 462 (quoted) and No. 541.

MADRIGALES / MADRIGALS: Maurer dates this *suite* to July or August 1922.

Alan S. Trueblood has written perceptively of the contrast between the straight line and the concentric circle in Lorca's imagery. (See the discussion in the Introduction.) Lorca develops a contrast between one who dreams (and writes verse) and a man of action pursuing a straight line. Implicitly the dreamy attitude courts frustration (as the image of the still water implies). A theme that will resurface in his play *Once Five Years Pass*, in the difficulty the young man has of defending a masculinity that is compatible with his being a poet. See Quance, 'Proyecciones en la pared del futuro' (in Bibliography).

CASTILLO DE FUEGOS ARTIFICIALES... / CASTLE OF FIREWORKS...: Ms dated 8 August 1922, revised in 1926.

'Catherine Wheel': A kind of pinwheel firework, named after the 'breaking' wheel, on which, according to legend, St Catherine was tortured. The story is recounted in a medieval work on the lives of the saints which Lorca and others of his generation knew well, *The Golden Legend* by Jacobus de Voragine (1229–1298).

'Game of moons': The title of the original, 'Juego de lunas', can also be translated as 'Set of Moons.'

The motif of the arrow and the eyes returns in a visual form in one of

Lorca's later surrealist drawings, 'San Sebastian' (1927), where arrows converge on the poet's face, which is only suggested by his one open eye and mouth.

SURTIDORES / WATER JETS: An undated ms. Maurer traces it tentatively to November 1922, though perhaps going back to the summer of 1921 (*CP* 709).

This *suite* is incomplete. A page which would have contained the beginning of the poem that comes just before 'Garden' is missing. The ms was published in facsimile *in Surtidores. Algunas poesías inéditas de Federico García Lorca*, ed. Paul Rogers (México: Editorial Patria, 1957).

Strictly speaking, a *surtidor* is a water jet, and the poet has its verticality very much in mind. It is an image used by some *modernistas* and then resignified by *ultraístas*. If I have opted for 'fountain' at points it is because the word falls better on the ear and can, at the same time, imply a basin that catches the falling water. Lorca took the first poem 'Interior' and included it in *Canciones* under the title 'Granada y 1850'.

'Interior': In line 3 I am correcting what, according to Jaime Sánchez Romeralo, appears to be an erroneous rendering of the ms, which has been been read as 'Un dedo de la parra ('grapevine) instead of 'la parca' (fate). This error has been reproduced in subsequent editions of Lorca's poetry. See 'En torno a la canción "Granada y 1850" de Federico García Lorca', *Homenaje a Alonso Zamora Vicente, Tomo IV, Literatura española de los siglos XIX y XX* (Madrid: Castalia, 1994), 363–85.

'Country': A specialized sense of *país* refers to the painted cloth on a folding fan. The poem might thus metaphorize a representation that is only seen obliquely, as one would see the picture on a fan that is being opened and shut.

'Garden': Lorca's poem is steeped in the symbolism of traditional verse dating from the Medieval period, such as the well-known 'Dentro del vergel': 'Dentro del vergel / moriré // Dentro del rosal / matarme han' [Inside the garden I will die // Inside the rose garden I will be slain]. He quoted the poem in full in his 1933 lecture 'Juego y teoría del duende' (*OC* IV, 150–62). Hence the allusion to 'knights' and to the rose, the emblem of a maiden's virginity.

The reader should note that the last line in the poem is a plural command:

'you all'; everyone is advised to stay away from the garden of love and the roles that lovers play. For more on this, see Quance, *In the Light*, 46–59

In a text from 1923–1924 offering advice to the young poet Lorca writes: 'Aprende del surtidor que estremece misteriosamente los jardines nocturnos y nadie sabe cuándo llora o ríe, cuándo empieza ni cuándo acaba' (*OC* III, 293) [Learn from the water-jet, which makes the gardens shiver mysteriously at night; no one knows when it cries or when it laughs, when it begins, or when it ends].

HERBARIOS / HERBALS: The original ms has been lost. The *suite* was first published in Mexico in December 1938, in the journal *Taller*. Maurer (*CP* 909) suggests December 1922 as its date.

Antonio Machado has a poem (S. LI) devoted to the herbal: 'Tengo dentro de un herbario / una tarde disecada' [I have a desiccated evening / inside an herbal...], lines in which it is clear that his romantic sentiment has faded. Like Lorca, Machado plays with the idea that although the voice from the past has fallen silent, it can be heard again on the pages of pressed flowers. See Antonio Machado, *Poesía y prosa*, Vol II, critical edn by Oreste Macrí (Madrid; Espasa Calpe/Fundación Antonio Machado, 1989), 804. The poem was published in 1924, according to the editors. See p. 1001.

The cosmic themes found throughout the *suites* imply flight from a present of frustrated love and desire. By taking the longest perspective imaginable in terms of both space and time, the poet manages to make the object of desire shrink and almost disappear from view.

SNAIL: Ms dated November 1922, revised 1926 (Maurer *CP* 909).

Spanish readers will be aware of the traditional children's rhyme: *Caracol col col, Saca tus cuernos al sol. Que tu padre y tu madre también los sacó.* [Snail, little snail, bring your horns out in the sun. / For that is what your father and your mother had done]. This little ditty celebrates the fact that when the sun shines after the rain, the snails will venture to poke their heads out of their shells.

In the first poem in the sequence the implication is that any outward movement might mean abandoning a private dream (the inwardness figured by concentric circles and spirals.) On the other hand, the urge to move straight ahead – like a cry on the wind – is hard to suppress. The second poem picks up the contrast again.

See Giovanni Caravaggi on this *suite* (in Bibliography). The image of the child who wants to be let out of the poet's heart is linked to the last *suite*, in which the poet is haunted by his unborn children, and also to the 1931 drama *Once Five Years Pass*, which Lorca was still hoping to debut in 1936 before the outbreak of war.

EN EL BOSQUE DE LAS TORONJAS DE LUNA / IN THE WOOD OF LUNAR GRAPEFRUITS: This is one of two drafts of the final *suite* and generally taken to be the earlier of the two, though the date cannot be pinpointed. (See Introduction.) In this version of the *suite* the poet introduces an image that we do not find in the longer one but which is, arguably, an allusion to the 'lunar grapefruits' of the title – metaphorized as silver disks on the trees in his garden, a fruit that grows by moonlight. Spanish folksong offers the choice of oranges or lemons to prospective (heterosexual) lovers (marriage and children or celibacy, unrequited love). The word *toronja* may be considered a regional variant of the fruit we know as an orange. It is interesting to note that in a folktale collected by Agustín Durán, *Leyenda de las tres toronjas del vergel de amor* (Madrid: n.p., 1856), the three components of the story: a *vergel* (a luxuriant garden), love, and 'oranges' are all present. The hero is a knight who seeks to free bewitched princesses from the fruit in which they are imprisoned. Lorca returns to this odd idea in a playful rhyme from 'Vals en las ramas' [Waltz in the Trees] in *Poet in New York*: 'The nun (*monja* / was singing in the orange (*toronja*)' (*OC* I, 570).

I have followed Miguel García-Posada's edition of the *suite* in the *OC* III, 833–59, which he has placed in the Notes. Maurer, like Belamich before him, offers it as another, earlier version with a validity of its own.

The variation in the title – garden or wood – shows a hesitancy about how to name the hero's destination. A garden is a protected space; a wood might pose more challenges and openly court myth. With its witches and dragons and keepers of the tower, this version of the final *suite* builds a fairytale atmosphere. Lorca appears to have opted for the more hermetic vision in his Garden version. See Quance, *In the Light of Contradiction* for more discussion.

Epigraph: Pero López de Ayala (1332–1407) is a medieval poet and historian.

'Reflection': In line 7 'no menees' (lit. do not shake).

'The Three Undeceiving Witches': Like Shakespeare's weird sisters, they preside over destiny and the beginning of life, hence the reference to a timeless gloom that is the 'kingdom of the seed'. The poet takes us back to a point 'antes de la vida', according to Charles Marcilly ('Las Suites', p. 45), when all life is a theory. In insisting that the witches are 'undeceiving' or truth-saying, and that they are the 'enemies' of the rainbow, the poet begins on a sober, metaphysical note. I wanted to preserve the Renaissance connotations here, in contrast to the alternative translation 'disillusioning', for Shakespeare's witches of *Macbeth* hover over the scene.

Line 10: The original *primeros planos* might be more literally the first captures or shots taken of something, or what is perceived in the foreground of a picture.

[fragment]: 'Swallow or spit out the mouthful / Adam took.' Here there is a clear allusion to original sin, but the stark alternatives suggest that the intellectual context is early Church doctrine, which took a dour view of the need for marriage and sexual reproduction.

'Tower': The Father-time figure in the tower (HIM) invokes the narrator's as a soul that is 'crippled but crystal-clear', a line reminiscent of Lorca's claim in an early autobiographical text that his childhood soul was 'de cristal' (*OC* IV, 843).

EN EL JARDÍN DE LAS TORONJAS DE LUNA / IN THE GARDEN OF THE LUNAR GRAPEFRUITS: Existing documentation places this *suite* in July and August of 1923. But, as explained in the Introduction, the order and even some of the contents of the *suite* are conjectural. The extant mss show extensive revision and some poems are blocked off, as if to signal that upon revision the poet proposed to exclude them. This is the case with 'Arbour', for example, and 'The White Satyr'.

Different sources have been proposed for the image of the garden. Maeterlinck was first named as a possible inspiration for the walled garden (Dinverno, *Listening*, 231–32), but the imagery is also elucidated by reference to Hans Christian Andersen, 'The Story of a Mother', with its God-like gardener in charge of every soul in his plot. Lorca's garden is an other-worldly one situated outside a cycle of birth and death, whence souls emerge. The poet appears to have fused a reading of Maeterlinck and Schopenhauer in imagining a silent garden where lovers either meet and conceive a child or pass each other by, if they are not meant to be. See Quance, *In the Light of Contradiction*, 65–72 and 'Proyecciones en la pared del porvenir: hacia *Así que pasen cinco años*' (in Bibliography).

In an early (unfinished) piece for the theatre, '[Diálogo con Luis Buñuel]' (around 1924) Lorca says, unlike his friend for whom travel (and its adventure?) is an 'obsession', 'I, on the other hand … prefer to travel in my garden'. A third friend in the dialogue suggests optimistically that both points of view, looking outward or inward, are valid. See *OC* II, 637. However, in his lecture on the Baroque poet Pedro Soto de Rojas, 'Paraíso cerrado para muchos, jardines abiertos para pocos' [A paradise closed to the many, gardens open to the few], Lorca suggests that the 'thirst for adventure leads to death'; and that therefore it is wiser to 'hold back (*ceñirse*) and travel in one's garden', that is, it is better to look within oneself for the Golden Fleece. See *OC* III, 78–87 (p. 86).

'Perspective': I follow Dinverno (*Listening*, 276) in reading 'descarriadas' (misguided, wayward, gone astray) instead of 'desconocidas' in line 14 in the fourth stanza. The ms bears this out.

'White Scent': Of the two paths alluded to, one is that of the sacrificed young maiden, like St Olalla of the ballad 'Martirio de Santa Olalla' [Martyrdom of St Olalla] in the *Romancero gitano* [Gypsy Songbook] / Her severed breasts suggest a sexuality that will not include motherhood.

The other is the path of a young woman wearing a dress with a long train – a bridal gown, perhaps – who can expect to have children. The Image of the Milky Way goes back to a myth about Juno and her breast milk splashing to create the stars in the galaxy.

'Encounter', line 21: 'The branches thicken…' a reminder that this encounter may take place in a wood; line 22: 'Neither one of us has been born'. See Lorca's lament about his 'artificial self' in a letter to Regino Sainz de la Maza quoted in the note on *The Forest of Clocks*.

'Dunes': To go back to his 'living birds' is a strong hint that this last *suite* involves a poet's search for words. In his lecture on Góngora ('La imagen poética de don Luis de Góngora', 1926), Lorca uses the metaphor of an (internal) night hunt to speak of the writing of poetry: 'The poet who is going to write a poem within his imaginative field has the vague sensation that he is going on a nocturnal hunt in a far-off wood' (*OC* III, 65).

Christopher Maurer (*CP* 911) calls our attention to an alternative ending to this poem, found in a ms dated 1 August 1923: 'El jardín seguirá / en la orilla del tiempo / golpeando furioso / la puerta de la Vida'. [The garden will go on/on the shores of time / pounding furiously / at the door of Life.] The other-worldly garden is where life originates. In 'The Story of a Mother' Hans Christian Andersen develops a fairy tale with the motif of a garden where each soul in the world grows. The alternate lines would take the reader back to the prologue, where the Narrator insists that there are 'points of light' pounding on the wall of the world in order to gain entry.

'Dawn and Pealing Bells': A *cielo bajo* is a low sky, near to the earth; meant briefly as a title for the projected 1926 edition of the *suites*.

The ms, which is dated 1 August 1923, gives the last two lines as follows: 'Alma mía, pon a oreo / Tu colección de palabras!' (roughly: Soul, let the air freshen / your collection / of words). It is not the opposite of imposing silence on himself but an urge, perhaps, to close the subject. The poet-narrator's insistence that his soul is both male and female dovetails with hermetic belief and at the same suggests a dissenting sexuality.

APPENDIX

[YO] / [I]: Ms dated 10 December 1920.

This sequence – which García Posada reserves for a category of 'less finished suites' *OC* I, 975) and which Maurer does not include in his *CP* – makes it clear that Lorca felt the need, when he set about modernizing his work, to define his own poetics against some of the more radical 'modernalatrous' manifestos. The place of the I (*yo*) in verse was much debated by avantgardists. Although the trend was toward an object-oriented poetry, and some young writers such as Borges felt that there was no substance to the self, one of the *ultraísta* manifestos signed off by Guillermo de Torre was in favour of the strong I as the mark of the original creator. See his 'Estética del yoismo ultraísta" [*Cosmópolis*, No. 29, May 1921] – a Nietzschean cry for the triumph of individuality. The manifesto was read at the first *ultraísta* evening at the Parisiana Club in

Madrid on 28 January 1921. For the rest, Lorca plays with the alphabet just as Gómez de la Serna did in his *Greguerías*. associating each letter with an object or animal. In the ms Lorca exaggerates the size of the Y in each of the titles, as if to draw a winnowing-fork.

DIURNO / DIURNAL DIPTYCH: This poem is dated 10 December 1920. García-Posada reserves it for a section containing the 'less finished' *suites* (*OC* I, 702), while Maurer places it in an Appendix (*CP*, 434). In a letter to Melchor Fernández Almagro (around the end of June 1921) Lorca writes:

> I believe my place is among those musical poplars [of the *vega* in Granada] and those constantly pooling, lyrical rivers, because my heart rests there in a definitive way and I laugh at the passions that are harassing me like a pack of panthers in the *tower* of the city (emphasis added, *E* 119]

The diptych dates from Lorca's first exposure in Madrid to the avant-garde and in particular to Ultraism, whose motto *Ultra* means 'beyond' in Latin. The ms includes a dedication to the *ultraísta* leader Guillermo de Torre, which may have been entered a few years after the poem was composed. Torre and others exalted the city and technology, while Lorca prefers traditional wisdom.

The allusions to the tortoise should remind readers of fables such as Aesop's 'The Tortoise and the Hare'. As for the tower, many avant-gardists epitomized modernity in the image of the tower, beginning with Robert Delaunay's celebrated painting of the Eiffel Tower (1911). In 1917 Vicente Huidobro wrote a long poem inspired in the Eiffel Tower as well.

The image of grass growing unchecked is one that Lorca repeatedly associates with death, as in the poem 'Ruin' from *Poet in New York:* 'I saw the blades of grass arrive / and I threw a bleating lamb / at their sharp little teeth and lancets' (*OC* I, 551).

'Reaction': 'De pontifical…' – dressed for certain Church ceremonies requiring a cape (in the shape of a tortoise's shell) which is known as a *cope*

NOCHE / NIGHT: From a ms dated 10 January 1921. The circus motif, with metaphors drawn from the nighttime sky, links this poem to the *suites*, as does the motif of the heart that is in peril. In the original

Spanish a somersault is a *salto mortal* (mortal jump) to the beyond – to an encounter with love?

[EL CAMPO SEGADO] / [MOWN FIELD]: This poem, which has perhaps broken off from one of the *suites*, draws on imagery that is central to *In the Garden of Lunar Grapefruits*, though no one to date has ventured to find a place for it there. In the poem 'Perspective', for example, the seeds in a visionary garden are said to dream that they will blossom.

Here the world 'is an ideal blue one that rises up *after* a field of wheat has been harvested, as if to replace the daylight world, or as if the 'death' of the seeds now released their dreams' (Quance, *In the Light*, 97).

TIERRA CIELO / EARTH SKY: This little poem, which Lorca mentions in a letter of 30 July 1923 (*E* 204), was incorporated into Christopher Maurer's edition of *In the Garden of Lunar Gapefruits* (*CP* 408–409), but not in the version offered by García-Posada in the *Obras completas*. We do not know where Lorca would have placed it. He eventually moved the poem to *Canciones*, where it appeared under a new title 'Friso' [Frieze], in the *OC* I, 353. Its connection to the theme of the mismatched lovers in 'Garden Pictures' is evident.

[A CHILD HAS JUST BEEN BORN]: An undated ms which may be linked to Lorca's last *suite* from 1923. Belamich noted that the following lines had been written on the back: 'When a child is born / there is a quaking / in the cold wood'.

Line 3: 'my crystal drops' suggests the speaker's tears

Line 15: 'The child is my sheep' is a phrase that echoes in Act 3 of *The House of Bernarda Alba*, when Bernarda's mad mother sings of a child in these terms: 'Little sheep, my little child, / let us go down to the seashore' (*OC* III, 628). In Lorca's theatre having a child of one's own is inseparable from an often impossible expression of desire.

SELECTED BIBLIOGRAPHY

The following gathers works referred to in the Introduction and Notes. I have also included works which address critical issues in Lorca's songs and *suites* and works that help contextualize the poetics.

Abbreviations

ALEC *Anales de la literatura española contemporánea*
BHS   *Bulletin of Hispanic Studies*
FGL   *Boletín de la Fundación Federico García Lorca*

Editions and Anthologies

Anderson, Andrew and Christopher Maurer, eds, *Epistolario completo* (Madrid: Cátedra, 1997).

Belamich, André, ed., *Federico García Lorca. Suites* (Barcelona: Ariel, 1983).

García-Posada, Miguel, ed., *Federico García Lorca. Obras completas.* 4 vols (Barcelona: Círculo de Lectores/Galaxia Gutenberg, 1995–1996).

Hernández, Mario, ed., *Libro de los dibujos de Federico García Lorca* (Madrid: Tabapress and the Fundación Federico García Lorca, 1990).

Martin, Eutimio, ed., *Federico García Lorca. Antología comentada (I, Poesía)* (Madrid: Ediciones de la Torre, 1988).

Maurer, Christopher, ed., *Federico García Lorca. Complete Poems.* 1st rev. edn (New York: Farrar, Straus and Giroux, 2002).

Menarini, Piero, ed., *Canciones y Primeras canciones* (Madrid: Espasa Calpe-Clásicos Castellanos, 1986).

Rogers, Paul, ed., *Surtidores. Algunas poesías inéditas de Federico García Lorca* (Mexico: Editorial Patria, 1957).

Soley, Ramon, ed., *Ferias* (Barcelona: Editorial Delstre's, 1997).

Soria Olmedo, Andrés, ed., *Federico García Lorca, En el jardín de las toronjas de luna* (Seville: Renacimiento, 2008), 95–122 [general anthology with different edition of last *suite*].

On Lorca

Anderson, Andrew A., 'Lorca at the Crossroads: "Imaginación, inspiración, evasión" and the "novísimas estéticas"', *ALEC* 16 (1991), 149–73.

Anderson, Andrew A., '¿Entre prodigio y protegido? El joven Lorca en Madrid (1919–1920)', *FGL* 17 (June 1995), 91–101.

Assumma, Maria Cristina, *La voce del poeta. Federico Garcia Lorca. L'oralità e la tradizione popolare* (Roma: Artemide, 2007).

Babín, María Teresa, 'The Voice of Nature in the Life of the Water (García Lorca's Vision from 1923 to 1936)', in *The World of Nature in the Works of Federico García Lorca*, ed. Joseph Zdenek (Rock Hill, SC: Winthrop College, 1980), 139–50.

Belamich, André, 'Las *Suites* en la vida y la obra de Lorca', in *Lecciones sobre Federico García Lorca*, ed. Andrés Soria Olmedo (Granada: Edición del Cincuentenario, 1986), 267–76.

Bonaddio, Federico, ed., *A Companion to Federico García Lorca* (London: Tamesis, 2007).

Bonaddio, Federico, *Federico García Lorca. The Poetics of Self-Consciousness* (London: Tamesis, 2010).

Bonet, Juan Manuel, 'Quince instantáneas lorquianas (y una coda postumista) in *Teoría del duende*', ed. Enrique Juncosa (Granada: Centro Fundación Federico García Lorca), 83–120.

Bosch, Rafael, 'Los poemas paralelísticos de Federico García Lorca', *Revista Hispánica Moderna* 28 (1962), 36–44.

Caravaggi, Giovanni, 'Struttura e poesia di una "diferencia" lorchiana: la Suite del Caracol', in *L'imposibile/posibile di Federico García Lorca*, Atti del convegno di studi, Salerno, 9–10 maggio 1988 (Naples: Pubblicazioni Degli Studi di Salerno/ Edizioni Scientfiche Italiani, 1989), 59–75.

De la Ossa Martínez, Marco Antonio, 'García Lorca: La música y las canciones populares españolas', *Alpha (Osorno)* (39) (2014), 93–121. https://dx.doi.org/10.4067/S0718-22012014000200008.

Dennis, Nigel, 'Lorca in the Looking-Glass: On Mirrors and Self-Contemplation', in *'Cuando yo me muera': Essays in Memory of Federico García Lorca*, ed. C. Brian Morris (Lanham, MD, New York and London: University Press of America, 1988), 41–55.

De Long Tonelli, Beverly, '"In the Beginning Was the End": Lorca's New York Poetry', *ALEC* 12 (1987), 243–57.

Diego, Gerardo, 'Federico García Lorca. Canciones. *Suplementos de Litoral*', *Revista de Occidente* 51 (September 1927), 380–84, reprinted in *FGL* 2 (December 1987), 42–45.

Dinverno, Melissa, 'García Lorca's Suites and the Editorial Construction of Literature', *Modern Language Notes* 119, 2 (2004), 302–28.

Dinverno, Melissa, *Listening through Mirrors. Representing García Lorca's Suites* (unpublished doctoral dissertation, University of Michigan, 2000).

Eich, Christoph, *Federico García Lorca, poeta de la intensidad*, 2nd rev. edn (Madrid: Gredos, 1976).

Feal Deibe, Carlos, *Eros en Lorca* (Barcelona: Edhasa 1973).

Fernández Cifuentes, Luis, ed., *Estudios sobre la poesía de Federico García Lorca* (Madrid: Istmo, 2005)

Fuentes, Tadea, *El folklore infantil en la obra de Federico García Lorca* (Granada: Servicio de Publicaciones de la Universidad de Granada, 1990).

Gala, Candelas, 'Lorca's *Suites*: Reflections on Cubism and the Sciences', *BHS* 80 (2003), 509–24.

Gala, Candelas, *Poetry, Physics and Painting in Twentieth-Century Spain* (Basingstoke, Hampshire: Palgrave Macmillan, 2011).

García Lorca, Francisco, *Federico y su mundo*, ed. and prol. Mario Hernández (Madrid: Alianza, 1980).

García Montero, Luis, *El lector llamado Federico García Lorca* (Madrid: Taurus, 2016).

Gibson, Ian, *Federico García Lorca. I: De Fuente Vaqueros a Nueva York 1898–1929* (Barcelona: Grijalbo, 1985).

Gibson, Ian, *Federico García Lorca. II: De Nueva York a Fuente Grande 1929–1936* (Barcelona: Grijalbo, 1985).

Gibson, Ian, 'Lorca's "Balada triste": children's songs and the theme of sexual disharmony in "Libro de poemas"', *BHS* 46, 1 (1969), 21–38.

Gibson, Ian, *Lorca y el mundo gay. 'Caballo azul de mi locura'* (Barcelona: Planeta, 2009).

Gil, Ildefonso-Manuel, ed., *Federico García Lorca* (Madrid: Taurus, 1973).

Harris, Derek, ed., *The Spanish Avant-Garde* (Manchester: Manchester University Press, 1994).

Hernández, Mario, ed., 'Introducción'. *Canciones 1921–1924* (Madrid: Alianza, 1982), 11–25.

Hernández, Mario, 'Introducción'. *Primeras canciones. Seis poemas galegos. Poemas sueltos. Colección de canciones populares antiguos* (Madrid: Alianza, 1981), 11–47.

Herrero, Javier, 'La crisis juvenil de Lorca: el pulpo contra la estrella', *Actas del X Congreso de la Asociación Internacional de Hispanistas*, 21–26 de agosto de 1989 (Barcelona: Promociones y Publicaciones Universitarias, 1992), 1825–34.

Juncosa, Enrique, ed., *Teoría del duende*, exhibition catalogue, 30 October 2015–10 January 2016 (Granada: Centro Federico García Lorca, 2015).

Loughran, David K., *Federico García Lorca. The Poetry of Limits* (London: Tamesis, 1978).

Machado, Antonio, *Poesía y prosa*, Vol. II, critical edn by Oreste Macrí (Madrid; Espasa Calpe/Fundación Antonio Machado, 1989).

Marcilly, Charles, 'Las *Suites* de Federico García Lorca. El jardín de las simientes no florecidas', *Revista de Occidente* 65 (October 1986), 33–50.

Maurer, Christopher, *Federico García Lorca y su 'Arquitectura del cante jondo'* (Granada: Comares, 2000).

Maurer, Christopher, 'García Lorca y el ramonismo', *FGL* 5 (1989), 55–60.

Mayhew, Jonathan, *Apocryphal Lorca* (Chicago: University of Chicago Press, 2009).

Menarini, Piero 'Las fuentes de *Canciones* (1927) de Federico García Lorca', in *Federico García Lorca et Cetera. Estudios sobre las literaturas hispánicas en honor de Christian de Paepe*, eds Nicole Delbecque, Nadia Lie, and Brigitte Adriaensen (Leuven UP, 2003), 159–70.

Min, Yong-Tae, 'Lorca, poeta oriental', *Cuadernos Hispanoamericanos* 358 (April 1980), 129–44.

Morris, C. B., *Son of Andalusia. The Lyrical Landscapes of Federico García Lorca* (Liverpool: Liverpool University Press, 1997).

Newton, Candelas, 'Proyecciones de "El jardín de las toronjas de luna" de García Lorca', *Hispanic Journal* 5, 2 (1984), 101–12.

Orringer, Nelson, 'El impacto del creacionismo en *Canciones* de García Lorca', *RILCE Revista de Filología Hispánica* 24, 2 (2008), 357–74.

Ortiz Saralegui, Juvenal, 'Federico García Lorca y Rafael Barradas', *Romance* [Mexico] 19 (18 December), 9.

Ortuño Casanova, Rocío, 'Dos o tres soluciones poéticas a la fugacidad del tiempo en las *Suites* de Lorca', *Hispanic Research Journal* 12, 4 (2011), 323–42.

Otero Seco, Antonio, 'Una conversación inédita con Federico García Lorca. Indice de la obra inédita que dejó el gran poeta', in *Obras completas* III, 625–27.

Peral Vega, Emilio, *Pierrot/Lorca. White Carnival of Black Desire* (London: Tamesis, 2015).

Perri, Dennis, 'Lorca's Suite *Newton:* the Limits of Science and Reason', *Hispanófila* 34, 101 (1991), 25–36.

Perri, Dennis, 'Lorca's Suite "Palimpsestos": Keeping the Reader at Bay,' *Romance Quarterly* 38, 2 (1991), 197–211.

Quance, Roberta, *In the Light of Contradiction. Desire in the Poetry of Federico Garcia Lorca* (Oxford: Legenda, 2010).

Quance, Roberta, 'Lorca's *Canciones*: The Poetics of Desire', in *Selected Proceedings 32nd Mountain Interstate Foreign Language Conference*, ed. Gregorio C. Martín (Winston Salem North Carolina: Wake Forest University, 1984), 255–63.

Quance, Roberta, 'Lorca's Liminal Poetics: *In the Garden of the Grapefruits of the Moon*', in *Liminal Poetics, or the Aesthetics of Dissent*, ed. Belén Piqueras (Madrid: The Gateway Press, 2008), 97–115.

Quance, Roberta, 'Proyecciones en "la pared del futuro": hacia *Así que pasen cinco años*', in *Teoría del duende*, ed. Enrique Juncosa (Granada: Fundación García Lorca, 2015), 134–50.

Quance, Roberta, 'The Trouble with Gender in Lorca's Suites: 'Surtidores', *Hispanic Review* 74, 4 (2006), 397–418.

Quance, Roberta, 'Women in High Places: Two Allegories in Lorca's *Primeras canciones*', *Revista canadiense de estudios hispánicos* 20.2 (1996), 285–303.

Román Román, Isabel, 'Los mitos clásicos en la poesía de Federico García Lorca', *Anuario de Estudios Filológicos* 26 (2003), 387–405.

Sahuquillo, Angel, *Federico García Lorca y la cultura de la homosexualidad masculina* (Alicante: Instituto de Cultura 'Juan Gil Albert', 1991).

Salazar Rincón, Javier, 'Arco, yeso y cal: tres símbolos de la muerte en la obra de Federico García Lorca', *Epos* 14 (1998), 277–92.

Salazar Rincón, Javier, *'Rosas y mirtos de luna...'. Naturaleza y símbolo en la obra de Federico García Lorca* (Madrid: UNED, 1999).

Stainton, Leslie, *Lorca. A Dream of Life* (New York: Farrar Straus and Giroux, 1999).

Torre, Guillermo de, *Literaturas europeas de vanguardia* (1925; Seville: Renacimiento Biblioteca del Rescate, 2001).

Trueblood, Alan S., 'Imágenes geométricas en la poesía temprana de Lorca', in *La voluntad de humanismo. Homenaje a Juan Marichal*, eds Birute Ciplijauskaité and Christopher Maurer (Barcelona: Anthropos, 1990), 233–47.

Walters, D. Gareth, *Canciones and the Early Poetry of Lorca* (Cardiff: University of Wales Press, 2002).

Yahni, Roberto K., 'Algunos rasgos formales en la poesía de Lorca. Función del paréntesis', in *Federico García Lorca*, ed. Ildefonso-Manuel Gil (Madrid: Taurus, 1973), 217–36.

Yahni, Roberto K., 'García Lorca y el folklore imaginario', II Congreso Internacional de Literatura y Cultura Españolas Contemporáneas 3 al 5 de octubre de 2011, Buenos Aires, PDF available from http://www.memoria.fahce.unlp.edu.ar/trab_eventos/ev.2842/ev.2842.pdf.

Other

Alcántara, Fernando, 'La vida artística', *El Sol*, 15 February 1921, p. 3.

Alvarez de Miranda, Angel, *La metáfora y el mito* (Madrid: Taurus, 1963).

Andersen, Hans Christian, *Cuentos de Andersen*, trans. J. Roca y Roca (1881; Barcelona: Biblioteca 'Artes y Letras', 1908).

[Anon.], 'Exposición Rafael Alberti. En el Ateneo', *El Sol*, 20 March 1923, p. 4.

Apollinaire, Guillaume de, 'El espíritu nuevo y los poetas. Un estudio póstumo de Apollinaire', *Cosmópolis* 1 (1919), 17–28.

Arroyo, Cesar E., 'La nueva poesía en América', *Cervantes* (August 1919), 105–13.

Asenjo Barbieri, Francisco, *Cancionero musical de los siglos XV y XVI* (Madrid: Real Academia de Bellas Artes de San Fernando, 1890).

Aullón de Haro, Pedro, *El jaiku en España* (Madrid: Hiperion, 2002).

Barrera López, José María, *El ultraísmo en Sevilla*, 2 vols. (Seville: Alfar, 1987).

Bonet, Juan Manuel, ed. *Las cosas se han roto. Una antología de la poesía ultraísta* (Madrid: Vandalia, 2012).

Boretz, Elizabeth, *Mysterious Realms. Functions of Imagery in Traditional Spanish Lyric and Balladry* (Newark, Delaware: Juan de la Cuesta, 1998).

Borges, Jorge Luis, 'La lírica argentina contemporánea. Selección y notas', *Cosmópolis* No. 38 (1921), 640–51.

Culler, Jonathan, *Theory of the Lyric* (Cambridge, Mass.: Harvard University Press, 2015).

Cummins, John G., *The Spanish Traditional Lyric* (Oxford and New York: Pergamon, 1978).

Dali, Salvador, 'San Sebastián', *gallo* (No. 1, February 1928), 1–12, [facsimile edn].

Díaz-Mas, Paloma, *Romancero* (Barcelona: Crítica, 1994).

Diego, Gerardo, ed., *Poesía española contemporánea 1915–1931* (Madrid: Signo, 1931).

Durán, Agustín, *Leyenda de las tres toronjas del vergel de amor* (Madrid; n.p., 1856).

Frenk Alatorre, Margit, ed., *Corpus de la antigua lírica popular hispánica (siglos XV a XVII)* (Madrid: Castalia, 1987).

García Prada, Carlos, 'La poesía imaginista y el hai-kai japonés', *Revista Iberoamericana* 21, 41 (1956), 373–91.

García-Sedas, Pilar, *Joaquím Torres-García i Rafael Barradas: un diàleg escrit: 1918–1928* (Barcelona: Publicacions de l'Abadia de Montserrat, 1994).

Geist, Anthony Leo, *La poética de la Generación del 27 y las revistas literarias: de la vanguardia al compromiso 1918–1936* (Barcelona: Guadarrama, 1980).

Gómez de la Serna, Ramón, *El alba y otras cosas* (Madrid: Editorial 'Saturnino Calleja', 1923).

Gómez de la Serna, Ramón, *Total de greguerías*, 2nd edn (Madrid: Aguilar, 1962).

Guigon, Emmanuel, *La infancia del arte. Arte de los niños y arte moderno en España*. Exhibition catalogue, Museo de Teruel, 5 November–8 December; Logroño, Sala Amós Salvador, 13 December 1996–12 January 1997 (Teruel: Museo de Teruel; Logroño: Cultural Rioja. 1996).

Henríquez Ureña, Pedro, *La versificación irregular en la poesía castellana*, prol. Ramón Menéndez Pidal (Madrid: n.p., 1920).

[Huidobro, Vicente], [Foreword], *Creación/Création 1921–1924*, facsimile edn (Madrid: Museo Nacional Centro de Arte/Ministerio de Educacion, Cultura y Deporte, 2001).

[Huidobro, Vicente], 'Non serviam', in Videla, Gloria, ed. *El ultraísmo*, 206–208.

Jiménez, Juan Ramón, *Belleza* (en verso) (1917–1923) (Madrid: Juan Ramón Jiménez y Zenobia Camprubí de Jiménez Editores de su propia y sola obra, 1923).

Machado, Antonio, *Poesía y prosa*, 2 vols, ed. Oreste Macrí (Madrid; Espasa Calpe/ Fundación Antonio Machado, 1989).

Maeterlinck, Maurice, *El huésped desconocido*, trans. Germán Gómez de la Mata (Madrid: Calleja, 1918).

Maeterlinck, Maurice, *El tesoro de los humildes*, trans. Eusebio Heras (Valencia, n.p., 1914).

Menéndez Pidal, Ramón, *Discurso acerca de la primitiva poesía lírica española, leído en la inauguración del curso 1919 a 1920*. Ateneo Científico, Literario y Artístico de Madrid (Madrid: Jiménez y Molina, 1919).

Menéndez Pidal, Ramón, *Romancero hispánico* (*Hispano-portugués, americano y sefardí)*, 2 vols (Madrid: Espasa-Calpe, 1953).

Ortega y Gasset, José, *La deshumanización del arte y otros ensayos* (1925; Madrid: Alianza, 1998).

Ortega y Gasset, José, *'Esquema de Salomé', Indice* 1 (1921), facsimile edn (Madrid; José Esteban Editor/Ediciones El Museo Universal, 1987), 1–2.

Paz, Octavio, *El arco y la lira* (Mexico, D.F.: Fondo de Cultura Económica, 1957).

Peña, Manuel de la, *El ultraísmo en España* (Madrid: Librería Concesionaria Fernando Fe, 1925).

Pérez Bazo, Javier, ed., *La vanguardia en España. Arte y literatura* (Toulouse: Cric & Ophrys, 1998).

Platón, *Diálogos, III: Fedón, Banquete, Fedro* (Madrid: Gredos/ Biblioteca Clásica, 1986).

Quance, Roberta, 'Espacios masculinos/femeninos: Norah Borges en la vanguardia', *Dossiers feministes* [Valencia] 10 (2007), 233–48.

Reckert, Stephen, *Lyra Minima* (London: King's College, 1970).

Salazar, Adolfo, 'Proposiciones sobre el hai-kai', *La Pluma* 6 (1920), 269–71.

Sánchez Romeralo, Jaime, 'En torno a la canción "Granada y 1850" de Federico García Lorca', in *Homenaje a Alonso Zamora Vicente, Tomo IV, Literatura española de los siglos XIX y XX* (Madrid: Castalia, 1994), 363–85.

Schopenhauer, Arthur, *El amor, las mujeres y la muerte* (Valencia: Prometeo, 1966).

Santos Torroella, Rafael, 'Barradas y el clownismo' in Rafael Barradas, exhibition catalogue (Madrid: Galería Jorge Mara, 1992), 25–33.

Tablada, José Juan, *Un día* (Caracas: Ed. Bolívar, 1919).

Torre, Guillermo de, 'Manifiestos Ultra. Estética del yoismo ultraísta', *Cosmópolis* No. 29, May 1921, 51–61.

Torre, Guillermo de, *Literaturas europeas de vanguardia* (1925; Seville: Renacimiento Biblioteca del Rescate, 2001)

Torre, Guillermo de, 'Los poetas cubistas franceses', *Cosmópolis* 12, 36 (1921), 603–28.

Torre, Guillermo de, 'Visita del "Interviewer Ignotus" al autor de *Hélices*', *Revista de la Casa América-Galicia* [later known as *Alfar*], facsimile edn, 28 April (1923), 236–38.

Videla, Gloria, *El ultraísmo. Estudios sobre movimientos poéticos de vanguardia en España*. 2nd edn (Madrid: Gredos, 1971).

INDEX OF TITLES AND FIRST LINES

English